Urban to the Core felt like a choral performance to me, with a number of voices singing the values, the prayers, and the stories that are at the heart of Urban Expression. We can be thankful to Juliet Kilpin for bringing this choir together and allowing them to sing with such honesty about their joys and small victories as well as their weaknesses, sorrows and questions. As you read through the twenty-one core values and the seven commitments of this wonderful organisation I trust you'll feel drawn into their song for the shalom of the city.
Michael Frost, Morling College, Sydney

I've lived and worked in the churches and communities of East London for forty-five years. Concerned about the Gospel in the inner cities, seeing the accelerating changes and now surrounded by scores of new churches in a multi-faith environment. From the experience of Urban Expression, skillfully gathered by Juliet Kilpin, comes something different and fresh. Get this book. Listen to the voices. Get behind the stories. Open your hearts. Use the prayers.
Colin Marchant, Urban Missiologist

At the outset learning is usually slow and laborious, but when someone shares their learning and experience in the generous and skilful way in the way Juliet Kilpin does, then the speed of learning can ramp up. Urban to the Core changes our perspective, showing how what once could only be dreamed of has become manifest. The honest thinking and holy intent expressed through these pages the wider secular world so often fails to see as being at the heart of Christian discipleship. The message that the Kingdom of God is both here and still to come is not just pious longing, Urban to the Core highlights the reality of this important insight.
Ann Morisy, Community Theologian

With captivating insight, honest vulnerability and profound wisdom Juliet reveals the depth of her own experience of urban living. With typical humility she illuminates the challenges and the beauty of the city and calls us to a greater engagement with both. Urban Expression excels at reflecting and learning alongside action and it is that combination which makes this a 'must read' for anyone engaged in urban mission.
Gary Bishop, Managing Director, Justlife

URBAN
TO THE CORE

MOTIVES FOR INCARNATIONAL MISSION

Juliet Kilpin

WIPF & STOCK · Eugene, Oregon

URBAN TO THE CORE
Motives for Incarnational Mission

Copyright © 2012 Juliet Kilpin. All rights reserved. Except for brief quotations in critical publications or reviews, no part of this book may be reproduced in any manner without prior written permission from the publisher. Write: Permissions, Wipf and Stock Publishers, 199 W. 8th Ave., Suite 3, Eugene, OR 97401.

First published in Great Britain by Matador, 9 Priory Business Park, Wistow Road, Kibwirth Beauchamp, Leicestershire. LE8 0RX, England.

Wipf & Stock
An imprint of Wipf and Stock Publishers
199 W. 8th Ave., Suite 3
Eugene, OR 97401
www.wipfandstock.com

ISBN: 978-1-62564-511-1

Manufactured in the U.S.A.

In memory of
Diane, Kathryn, Helen and Jane

Contents

Introduction	ix
Core Commitments	1
Core Values – Humility	58
Core Values – Creativity	101
Core Values – Relationship	152
What Now?	207
Appendix A: Biblical References	210
Appendix B: Get Involved	216
Bibliography	220

Introduction

Urban Expression started in 1997 when a team of eight young adults moved to East London with the shared conviction that the person and story of Jesus had potential to be really good news if communicated and incarnated relevantly. We observed that Jesus tended to operate on the margins and seemed to have a bias towards the poor and so chose one of the most under-churched and most deprived neighbourhoods of London at the time, Shadwell in Tower Hamlets.

This team, led by my husband Jim, and me, were not paid to do this but worked creatively to generate enough money to survive. We were not backed by any particular denomination or network of churches. In fact, our mission was perceived by many as somewhat whacky and irresponsible – such creative 'new forms of church' were not yet as fully endorsed in Britain as they appear to be fifteen years later. But we were supported by some of the most experienced urban practitioners of the time who formed a steering group to advise and nurture us.

For all we knew, Urban Expression could simply have stopped after that first team, but to our surprise we were swiftly followed by another team of seven moving into Stepney, a team of three moving into Wapping, a family unit moving into Forest Gate and a team of four moving into another part of Stepney, the Ocean Estate. Soon even more teams began across east and south-east London.

There was no blueprint, no model, no strategy and no process, but at its heart there were values and commitments that had been recognised in advance of our first team moving in. Rather than asking what we were going to *do* these values asked who we were going to *be*.

If you look at any organisation you can quickly determine what it is committed to. Whether these commitments have ever been verbalised or not, they will be seen in what the organisation or company does and how it does it. Think of companies like Google, Apple, Starbucks, Tesco and the like. What are they committed to? How do you know what they are committed to? They may state their mission clearly but it will be their delivery that convinces you about what really matters to them. A company that has a green policy but throws out substantial food waste, or one that insists it is in support of reducing unemployment but takes on slave labour, or one that theoretically supports the local economy but appears to offer local producers unfair prices because maximum profit is paramount, shows through its actions what it is truly committed to.

Urban Expression began with a desire to engage with marginalised communities through the creating and living out of Christian community in such places. We adopted the popular phrase 'church planting'. It is a term which means different things to different people and a term some of us feel more comfortable with than others. The reason it resonates differently is perhaps because the word 'church' implies a whole range of possible commitments to a whole range of different people.

When you think of 'church' as an organisation, a congregation, a community, a charity or however you have encountered it, what commitments are apparent to you? There may be positive and explicit commitments of which you are aware. For example, you may feel that 'church', as you know it, is committed to friendliness, serving the community, helping people explore faith, facilitating the worship of God, helping the poor, etc. There may also be less positive commitments which are unlikely to be written down anywhere but which may be implicit and easily recognisable. For example, the 'church' might be only for a certain type of person, might only take place on Sundays, might exclude people with certain lifestyles, might only be for those who like singing.

When Urban Expression was founded, we felt it was important to be explicit about some of our commitments and values, and to write these down. Without being explicit we feared we could drift, albeit unintentionally, into some of the implicit assumptions and expectations some might have of 'church'. Having our commitments and values written down would help us check how we were doing and would enable those who care for us to help us reflect on how well we were doing at living them out in reality, ensuring we never ended up talking about them but not living by them, as we so often see in global businesses.

As we explored and refined our commitments and values, we could see some patterns developing and natural groupings appeared. We have ended up with seven core commitments and twenty-one values which are grouped under three headings – Humility, Creativity and Relationship.

We do not claim to be perfect in living out these twenty-eight commitments and values. We are acutely aware of our imperfections and weaknesses, but we continue to hold these values as ideals we desire to walk intentionally towards. Those who see that we are not doing so are welcome to remind us of these ideals and help us reflect on how we can live them out more effectively.

Having been recognised at the very beginning, these values became the core of the interview and discernment process for team members, and their embodiment became the goal of each team. As teams morphed into expressions of Christian community in each neighbourhood, one might bear little resemblance to another and yet these core values could be seen clearly in what was taking shape in each community.

When one London team member decided to move home to Manchester, she asked if Urban Expression could start in her locality and so opened up the possibility of teams in other cities across Britain. And when one couple pioneering in The Hague visited a team in London, they became convinced that they were embodying the same values and asked if they could start Urban Expression in The Netherlands.

There has never been a global or even a national strategy, yet since 1997 there have been teams in London, Manchester, Glasgow, Birmingham, Bristol and Stoke; there are currently teams in Spoorwijk, Central Hague, Rotterdam, Arnhem and Amersfoort in The Netherlands; there is a team in Stockholm, Sweden and a team in Allentown, Pennsylvania plus various locally-based experimental expressions of urban mission on both U.S. coasts which are somewhat off the radar. To our surprise, by the end of our fifteenth year, in Britain alone there will have been around twenty teams of varying sizes and we will have recruited our one hundredth team member. All members give a minimum of three years to their team but most give more than that, and the vast majority of Urban Expression team members have remained in their inner-city neighbourhoods long term or have remained committed to the urban poor or those on the margins. We can currently count on one hand those who have left before their initial three-year commitment ended. We are not sure why our attrition rate is so low, but it may have something to do with the average time it takes for someone to decide to join a team (eighteen months). It is rarely a quick decision.

We do not feel like much of a success story – urban mission is gritty, demanding and hard work. None of the Christian communities we have pioneered look that successful according to common standards – they remain small, fragile and highly aware of their weaknesses and imperfections. Life often appears chaotic in the inner city. People's lives are astoundingly resilient yet deceptively delicate – too many people die early in the inner city. Urban life is so diverse, causing migraines and ecstasy in the one brain at the same time. However, in the rawness and grittiness of life there is creativity and freedom which is celebrated.

Yet, while we do not feel like much of a success, we want to take this opportunity to celebrate our teams and all that they have been and continue to be. We want to appreciate the communities they inhabit and learn the profound lessons they teach us. We want to honour the communities of faith and variety of initiatives that have sprung up which offer people solace, belonging and hope in places often marred by loneliness, anxiety and despair. We want to dig into the values that have founded us, that are our core, and explore how they are lived out in practice.

And so we offer you these short reflections on our values, brought to you by team members past and present. We are normal everyday people trying to follow Jesus. We are teachers, social workers, retail workers, students, accountants, youth workers, janitors, bus drivers, taxi drivers, chaplains, train drivers, drug counsellors, lecturers and nurses. We are brothers, sisters, sons, daughters, parents, addicts, sinners, lovers, haters who struggle with self-worth, identity and acceptance as much as anyone else. A few of us are also ordained 'ministers' in one denomination or another, but few are funded and most combine this with other employment of some kind.

As we celebrate our fifteenth year, this book offers some glimpses of the Urban Expression story so far. With grassroots, honest reflections from some of the one hundred UK-based team members past and present, what follows is an attempt to capture the essence of what has motivated and sustained this experimental urban mission agency. These reflections offer a variety of insights, some academic and theological, others personal and thoughtful; some abstract and creative, others practical and story-based.

If you are concerned about cities (over half the world lives in them now), or are interested in those on the margins of society, cross-cultural mission or new forms of church, you will make many connections with the story told in this book.

In the following pages I introduce each of our core commitments followed by our values which are divided into the three sections: Humility, Creativity and Relationship. My introductions are followed by one or two grass-roots reflections from team members which explore what the commitments and values look like when they are lived out.

Each reflection concludes with a prayer from our Urban Expression liturgy. These prayerful responses to the values have been creatively written by Sian Murray Williams to enable teams (and others) to interact regularly with them, enabling them to remain living values rather than a theoretical document. We hope you might find these simple, urban and earthed prayers helpful and inspirational. To conclude the book Stuart Murray Williams offers some personal reflections and asks 'What Now?'

Having been part of the first Urban Expression team back in 1997, and having been involved in the recruitment, deployment, networking and supporting of the subsequent teams, it has been a long-held desire of mine to gather some of the stories and share them. Every time someone makes the decision to join an Urban Expression team and move in to an urban neighbourhood I am moved by their courage, vulnerability and trust. I am inspired by their willingness to take a risk and commit to others in community. I am reminded that following Jesus is an exciting adventure, and being part of such an adventurous group of people gives me life.

It has been a pleasure gathering these reflections and I sincerely thank all the contributors who have taken the time to write their stories. I hope you are all encouraged as you listen back to the sounds of your collective voices that will inspire others to walk in your footsteps.

I also want to thank Stuart Murray Williams and Peter Sidebotham for their time and help in proof-reading this offering, giving much appreciated guidance, support and encouragement for this novice writer. Thanks also to Alan Collier for the title and cover ideas.

And most importantly I want to thank my husband and co-adventurer Jim, for guarding my sabbatical time to allow me to focus on this task, and for being the constant sounding-board for my numerous ideas, helping me discern the few that have potential to materialise into reality!

I offer you these tiny glimpses of the Urban Expression story in the hope that you might find inspiration and courage for the journey you are currently on and that you might take time to consider your own core values and practices in our increasingly urban world.

Juliet Kilpin
August 2012

For further information about Urban Expression please visit www.urbanexpresson.org.uk.

For information about our Crucible training course please visit www.cruciblecourse.org.uk.

You can download the Urban Expression liturgy booklet from www.proost.co.uk/urban-expression

For more on the first ten years of our story you can read *Church Planting in the Inner City: The Urban Expression Story*, by Juliet Kilpin and Stuart Murray (Grove Books, 2007).

Core Commitments

**We are committed to following God on the margins and in the gaps, expecting to discover God at work among powerless people and in places of weakness.**

All of us involved in Urban Expression are delighted that there is so much more creative and entrepreneurial mission taking place in the UK now. After decades of often replicating failing churches it seems there is now much more encouragement to start 'fresh expressions' or new forms of church. Some denominations seem to have got into the flow of this more than others – notably those whose demise is more apparent than others – but on the whole there is much more permission to experiment in this way. However, one frustration is that this still tends to happen on the ever-decreasing 'fringe' of the inherited church amongst those who look or behave 'most like us' and those who are 'nearest' to us in geography or mindset.

The truth, however, is that the vast majority of the British population is not very engaged with church at all, and so is on the margins because they are beyond the usual scope of church experience. And within this increasingly vast group there are those who often seem completely off the radar of most churches – they are the forgotten, the overlooked, the avoided and the uncomfortable ones.

Whilst it is encouraging to see creative work with those on the fringe of church life, Urban Expression is committed to going beyond that fringe to the margins. This is partly because this seems to be what Jesus prioritised and partly because both Old and New Testaments show God's kingdom breaking in from the margins more often than from the centre. And that's something we don't want to miss!

At Street Level

Louise Brown, formerly in Shadwell, London

I enjoyed seven years as part of an Urban Expression team based in Shadwell. Throughout this time God revealed himself to me through people whose lives were lived on the margins of society. Sharing in the lives of chaotic drug users reveals both the frailty and strength of human beings. Watching, and allowing my heart to be broken by their struggles to get clean and follow God was humbling. Seeing that God's love is not earned and his grace never runs out for people who, in an earthly sense, have little to give, has revealed to me how I live and operate as if I can earn God's love.

As I sat with a friend telling me of his struggles to stay clean, I recognised that I had no answers. I was powerless to help in his struggles. All I was able to do was listen and cry with him. Before Shadwell I had an answer to almost everything. Now I recognise my weakness and that apart from God we can do nothing. I then recognised that Christ came to earth as a helpless baby and died embracing his weakness upon the cross. One of his first miracles was to touch a leper living outside the city and restore him to his community.

The result of this was that Christ 'could no longer enter a town openly but stayed outside in lonely places' (Mark 1:45). Through touching the lives of others, often we are changed forever. Rather than coming to earth as a king in a crown, Christ died in the rubbish dump outside the Holy City. He lived and died in the gaps. Now I find myself at home in a Palestinian refugee camp and feel uncomfortable in established churches.

At times we were able to see God breaking into the gaps. One time I came out of hospital and friends had turned my home into a florist shop. A friend who was a prostitute was also staying with us for the week. Arthur (my husband) decided to buy her flowers too. Her face lit up as this was probably one of the only times a man had given her something without wanting anything in return. I believe she experienced, in that moment, something of God's unconditional love. She did not come to Christ through this and I have learnt that making Christians is not my place but God's. My place is to be where God wants me, showing his love and compassion. Our role as Christians is to obey Christ, how he chooses to use and bless this is his responsibility. This is incredibly freeing and allows me to sit in the margins with Christ, accept my weakness and embrace the weakness of others.

Astrid Milne, Leytonstone, London

In reflecting on what I understand by this value, I have found myself exploring different ways of interpreting it. I wonder if it could just as easily say:

We are devoted to walk behind God on the fringe and in the unfilled spaces, presuming to come across God's actions among helpless individuals and in situations of feebleness.

Following God, walking behind God, implies that He's been there before us. When 'He became flesh and moved into the neighbourhood' (John1:14, The Message), it was a poor part of town that He moved into. Our Lord Jesus was born in poverty to poor parents from an insignificant town, and thus, from the beginning Jesus identified Himself with those who were on the fringe of society. He made friends and shared His life with unimportant people like fishermen, and those frequently despised such as tax collectors and other 'sinners'. He went to the spaces that rabbis and the religious elite left unfilled, and there performed great acts of God's kingdom.

Or perhaps it could read:

We are dedicated to accompany/go around with God on the edge and in the rifts, believing to find and uncover God's deeds among vulnerable, defenceless souls and in areas of failing and shortcoming.

God has not only gone before us, but is also going with us. In the Great Commission Jesus reminded His followers that He will be with His disciples always, and we are committed to 'string along with' God in the power of the Holy Spirit. Jesus told His disciples that if they had faith they would do what He had been doing and even greater things (John 14:12). And Jesus had been anointed 'to preach the good news to the poor, to bind up the broken-hearted, to proclaim freedom for the captives and release from darkness for the prisoners' (Isaiah 61:1).

Or another version might say:

We apply ourselves to imitate and emulate God on the periphery and in the gulfs, assuming to see God's handiwork/service among impotent and ineffective persons and in positions of ineptitude.

Jesus spent time with people who society didn't really care about. Even now He's choosing 'the foolish things of the world to shame the wise;… the weak things of the world to shame the strong' (1 Corinthians 1:27). Sharing our lives, like Jesus did, with those who lead ineffective lives is a powerful tool in discipling them. Something as simple as sitting round the dinner table as a family with them, can be a real eye-opener to how different life can be when you are following Jesus.

Lord of the universe,
Lord of the smallest particle of dust,
we meet you in the broken and the despairing,
we know you in the unlikely and the unimagined.

We live alongside the bent and bruised
and we see you there;
We worship with the damaged and deranged
and we see you there;
We work with the oppressed and yearning
and we see you there;
and we meet our own fragmentation there too.

In encountering powerlessness
we see Jesus;
In our weakness
we meet Jesus;
In living with the gaps
we follow Jesus;
who is our power,
who is our strength,
who is our Lord,
and who leads us on.

You are working to make all things new
to help us to embody that hope,
to express that vision,
and to work for its coming.

Lord, in your mercy,
Let your kingdom come!

 We are committed to being Jesus-centred in our view of the Bible, our understanding of mission and all aspects of discipleship.

Urban Expression has frequently been referred to as an 'Anabaptist' mission agency. This is largely because the Anabaptist heritage tells the story of a marginalised group of Jesus followers who were content to work at the edges of society and prepared to disagree with the mainstream church (at substantial cost of life). We certainly draw inspiration from this heritage although only once we had written the values did we realise the similarities and enter conversation with others who shared Anabaptist tendencies!

Having a Jesus-centred view of the Bible is certainly a core Anabaptist outlook[1]. The decision to look at the Bible and society through the lens of Christ is one that gives freedom not only to ask the popular question 'what would Jesus do?' but the more foundational question 'what *did* Jesus do?' If Jesus, the Son of God, embodies the very nature and character of the triune God, then the way Jesus treated people, spoke with people, taught people, disciplined people and served people, can act as our litmus paper and role model.

As positively thought-provoking as the 'what would Jesus do' motto is, its weakness is that we can all try to guess what Jesus would do, but none of us will ever

---

1 For a full list of the Anabaptist Network core convictions visit www.anabaptistnetwork.com

know for sure how much our own political, national or cultural contexts impact our predictions. Would Jesus drive a BMW, have a mortgage, euthanise his mum, give money to an alcoholic, camp with the Occupy movement, join the Arab Spring, eat meat, be on Facebook, have a tattoo...? The answers to these and many more questions fill the ethics discussions of those who have substantially more time and brain space than me!

As immensely valuable and illuminating as these debates might be, we must ensure that they don't become an academic distraction from the core essence of the gospel, that is Christ. Across the nations, the tribes and the clans of this globe, we all have preconceived notions of what 'our' God is like. Yet the way Jesus lived and loved challenges all of our notions of the Divine, and if we can keep our eyes fixed on him, if we can ride the wave of divine discomfort and holy chaos that his life emanates and calls us to follow, we might grow to know God as fully as any sinful human can.

Vincent J Donovan reflects on his time as a missionary to the pagan Masai people of East Africa and suggests that 'a missionary's greatest contribution to the people for whom he works might well be to separate them from God, free them from their idea of God'[2]. So many of our notions of God become tribal. God is always on 'our side' (whoever 'we' are) and this seems often to give us the right to interpret academic ethical debates only in our favour. Yet Donovan challenges:

---

2 Donovan.V.J. *Christianity Rediscovered, An Epistle from the Masai* (SCM, 1978) p47

'The God that Jesus tells us of and shows us is so different from the God we had imagined with our own minds that it takes your breath away. If what Jesus says about God and shows us about God is true, then we can only say we would never have known about this God without Jesus'.[3]

We hope that by focussing on Jesus, those of us in Urban Expression will be a people who regularly have our breath taken away by him, and we hope that by introducing others to Jesus they will, like us, be able to become increasingly freed from tribal ideas of God and join us in the adventure of trying to understand and imitate what Jesus did.

At Street Level

Tim Presswood & Clare McBeath, Openshaw, Manchester

Walking in through the door was to walk straight into a solid wall of smoke. Mostly tobacco, but occasionally there was a whiff of something else. But not from Molly[4]. She chain-smoked, but nothing illegal. Not any more. Apart from her prescription-methadone, Molly was clean.

---

[3] Donovan.V.J. *Christianity Rediscovered, An Epistle from the Masai* (SCM, 1978) p73
[4] Names have been changed

Molly and her partner, Rick, lived across the road. Both addicts. Both suffering from a variety of AIDS-related afflictions. Rick was, by now, bed-ridden and Molly struggled to cope with the demands of three young children growing up in one of the most deprived and crime-ridden estates in the country.

Lee, in particular, was a constant source of worry. Bright as a button, he seemed to attract the attention of the local gangs, the police and, on at least two occasions, known paedophiles. Yet it was Lee who was often to be found in our little chapel, chatting with the old ladies. And it was Lee who decided that his mum and dad should get married before Rick died. And it was Lee who proudly walked his mum up the aisle, while his brother and sister walked with Rick as he staggered under his own steam to the front of the church to declare his love for this vulnerable woman.

Less than two months later, I was visiting Molly again, this time to arrange Rick's funeral. I needn't have bothered. Almost all our plans went astray as every junkie in the area decided to arrive an hour early – and the family decided that rather than wait for the hearse, they would carry Rick across the road into church.

The service was one of the most emotional outpourings of love that I have ever experienced. What I remember most, though, and still treasure, was the old – and possibly not entirely legitimate – VHS video of *The Borrowers*, which Molly insisted I take home for my daughter.

Several years went by. I would run into Molly – a little too often for comfort she was coming out of the local off-licence, but she would always have time for a kind word and a story of how Lee or one of the other children were doing. Lee still had his issues. His sister, Sonia, had a daughter at the age of just fifteen. His elder brother, Pete, got a job in Stockport. A job. Then Lee himself found a job in a Cheshire village. On another planet. We lost touch. I would occasionally see the increasingly frail Molly, hobbling around the streets. Until the day when, inevitably, I got the knock on the door. There were Lee, Sonia and Pete. The cancer which her body did not have the resources to fight, had finally got the better of Molly. Would I bury her, as I had buried Rick?

And as I looked on three clean, loving, straight-ish kids, I couldn't help but think back to that tobacco-filled first visit into Molly's home and wonder if, in her eyes, I had glimpsed the eyes of Jesus.

'I'm telling the solemn truth: Whenever you did one of these things to someone overlooked or ignored, that was me—you did it to me.' (Matthew 25:45, The Message)

Kenny Beaton, formerly in Shadwell, London

It may sound cheesy, but my time in London with the Urban Expression gang was simply life-changing and life-changing in the very best Jesus-centred way possible. We all attempted to be Jesus to each other and to those we attempted to serve in Shadwell. Our intention was to live out our lives according to the Bible and how we believe Jesus would want us to live and act to everyone we experienced. That in itself was a challenge. I believe I kind of got it easy while others around me really were put to the test in many, many challenging and difficult ways. It was, however, during these moments that we as a team really pulled together and supported and were Jesus to each other; and that for me was when the rubber hits the road, if you will. It was an honour to share life with the team(s) in East London in 1997 and onwards and to see Jesus and experience Jesus in the women and men and children of Urban Expression.

I remember the love and support the team gave me when I was attempting to become a bus driver! I was a nervous wreck, AN UTTER NERVOUS WRECK!! Without the support, love and prayers of my team, London's streets and pavements would NEVER have been safe! I remember Jules making a double-decker bus cake and being blown away by the gesture and although I was thinking 'I'm never gonna pass my bus test' I knew that whatever happened, I had the love and support of friends who loved and adored Jesus and I was never on my own and I could cope with anything that came my way.

I saw Jesus in Shadwell in Christians and non-Christians alike and experienced Jesus in places and ways I never thought possible. We helped disciple each other and those around us in the community in Shadwell and those memories and friends will stay with me forever and have helped shape my walk with my Abba, Jesus and the Holy Spirit.

Creator God,
we thank you for giving the Word
flesh and bones
in Jesus, our friend and brother.
In him we find our life,
we find our hope,
we find our joy.
In him we find out what it means
to be fully human.

We thank you for his centre
a life completely grounded in you.

We thank you for his compassion
which welled up uncontrollably
when he met brokenness.

We thank you for his vulnerability,
being fully alive in the hard places
with no protection, no defence.

We thank you for his playfulness
enjoying parties, good food and fine wine.

We thank you for his tenderness
in dealing with men and women.

We thank you for his vision of lives, the neighbourhood,
the country and the world
healed and whole,
filled with peace and justice.

We thank you for his sacrifice
that carried all the ugliness,
the bruised and battered stuff,
on a cross.

We thank you for raising him to life,
giving us a brand new place of standing
and through him a whole new future.

Lord, we long to be like Jesus.
Keep converting us,
and help us to be like Jesus
and walk with Jesus
through today
and this coming season.

Lord, in your mercy
Let your kingdom come!

 **We are committed to seeking God's kingdom in the inner city, both by planting churches and by working in partnership with others in mission.**

'God's church doesn't have a mission, God's mission has a church'. This phrase, popularised by the writings of David Bosch[5], spells out the meaning of the contemporary missiological term 'Missio Dei'. It looks posh in Latin, but it simply means 'God's mission'. Mission belongs to God. It is not 'primarily an activity of the church but an attribute of God'[6], it is and always has been God's idea and an adventure we are invited to be part of. Bosch explains 'Missio Dei' as:

> 'God's self-revelation as the One who loves the world, God's involvement in and with the world, the nature and activity of God, which embraces both the church and the world, and in which the church is privileged to participate.' [7]

'Missio Dei' suggests that the sending of God the Son by God the Father was an enacting of God's constant 'sending' of hope and good news, and the sending of God the Holy Spirit by God the Son was an enacting of all God's people being invited to be equipped and sent out for the same mission.

---

5 Bosch.D. *Transforming Mission* (Orbis, 1993)
6 Bosch.D. *Transforming Mission* (Orbis,1993) p390
7 Bosch.D. *Transforming Mission* (Orbis, 1993) p10

As such we believe that the kingdom of God takes precedence over the church. It is more important to be pursuing God's kingdom than to be in church. Just because you go to church doesn't mean you will automatically spot the work and movement of the kingdom and be involved. Yet if you pursue God's kingdom you will not be able to stop church happening in one form or another, 'there is church because there is mission, not vice versa'[8]. One might hope that the two would be synonymous, but sadly this is not always guaranteed. So we have made the seeking of God's kingdom a priority. We assume this will result in the creating of new Christian communities, but because God's kingdom is more important than our 'church planting strategy' (which we don't have!) we will not steam-roller over anyone or anything to achieve this task if God's kingdom seems to be moving in a different direction. We will also very happily work in partnership with others who are seeking God's kingdom as a mutual priority.

At Street Level

Ian Spence, Levensulme, Manchester

Ronnie said to me, 'Why is nothing happening round here for young people? The council are doing nothing, I wanna start a youth club!' My initial response was 'Great

---

8 Bosch.D. *Transfoming Mission* (Orbis, 1993) p390

idea'; I too had been thinking about some form of youth work, but I couldn't see how we could possibly staff it.

Ronnie is the sort of person who knows people, who know people who can source a snooker table! He knows people who are not youth work trained but would give an hour on a Friday to help. Having gathered a team, we spent some weeks gelling as a group, learning about youth work practice and processing CRB forms. Before long, we opened the doors and were soon inundated with young people who wanted somewhere to hang out.

There were challenges along the way, particularly in integrating Roma young people into the mixed ethnicity club. The club evolved and changed and gradually we established a good respectful relationship with the young people who in the early days had been running rings round us. But it was on a snowy Sunday morning that we realised the impact this youth work had made.

Completely of their own initiative the young people gathered early in the morning with salt and shovels to clear the path and ramp to the Baptist Church building which the youth club meets in. They had no intention of joining a service, and yet their service demonstrated Christ far more meaningfully than any hour of praise/worship and sermon could ever hope to achieve.

The young people's gathered community developed throughout the morning as they welcomed and helped younger children and church members to join in their service, and then they shared between them a packet of biscuits and small cups of Tizer! We are committed to seeking God's kingdom in the inner city…

We pray 'Let your kingdom come, Let your will be

done.' But do we take time to observe the answers to that prayer? The kingdom of God was there, outside that church building on that cold and slippery Sunday morning. The kingdom of God is there in the meeting and planning of community groups. It's there in the weekly luncheon meeting of the Bangladeshi elderly women's group. The kingdom of God is being enacted at the Sure Start centre, in the schools, in the High Street, in the back streets, in the maisonettes and tower blocks, in the terrace rows and yes sometimes even in our church buildings too. There are glimpses and magnificent demonstrations of the kingdom of God all around us and we need to recognise these, sometimes name them, always rejoice in them and, where appropriate, be prepared to play a part.

As we plant churches we seek God's kingdom rather than thinking we have some kind of exclusive ownership on it. Sometimes that sees us partnering with seemingly the most unlikely people or groups because the kingdom of God belongs to these. When Jesus is asked about the kingdom of God he uses parables and stories to try and describe what he's talking about, but you do sense something of Jesus' frustration at not being able to find the right language to do the kingdom justice. The kingdom of God is a bit like a mustard seed, although it's a bit like a lost coin… The kingdom of God is here, in our urban contexts (and in other areas too – we city people don't have exclusive ownership either!). The kingdom of God was seen in the breaking of biscuits and sharing of Tizer on a snowy cold morn.

Lord you surprise us in so many ways!
A smile from a person we hadn't even noticed;
A flower defying the ugliness around it;
A laugh heard from an open window;
The scent of a curry floating down the road;
The glory of a sunset lighting up the flats.
You are God!

You care for each person living here.
You love us overwhelmingly
and passionately.

You have invited us to be your people
of salt and light
and smiles and beauty
and joy and fragrance
a people who reflect your glory.

And you have invited us to work together with people like
us and people not like us.
Lord, show us what your
kingdom-shaped communities
can look like here;
encourage us in the building of them, and lead us into
deeper ways
of faithful and risky living.

In our yes to you,
keep our eye on the ball, on your love and purpose,
on your touch and word, on your life and energy,
for that is all we have and all we need.

Lord, in your mercy
Let your kingdom come!

 **We are committed to a vision of justice, peace and human flourishing for the city and all its inhabitants.**

The kingdom of God is important to us in Urban Expression. In the New Testament Jesus is quoted frequently talking about 'kingdom'. By 'kingdom' Jesus is referring to what the world would be like if God's rule was fully embraced – a world of justice and peace where humans live life in all its fullness.

In the Old Testament the same reality is described by the word 'shalom'. Traditionally translated as 'peace' it is a deep word which means so much more. It implies flourishing, completeness, wholeness, healing and everything being 'right', being the way it was always meant to be.

Across Urban Expression we believe that our role as God's co-workers in God's mission is to be those who point towards the anticipated kingdom, people who live out the longed-for shalom. This means seeking justice, being proactive peace-makers and seeking the welfare of those God has called us to live alongside, whether they think the same as us or not.

I remember in our early days sending a small group to Watney Market in Shadwell to do face-painting and give out balloons. It was not the first time we had done such activities in a community that was, at that time, rarely in receipt of such random generosity and joy. As I walked down the street, heading back home to collect something for the team, I was stopped by two women who asked in their broad Irish-Cockney accents "Ere, is that your lot up there doin all that stuff?'. 'Yes it is!' I replied, not knowing if they were going to commend or criticize. 'See I told you it would be them lot' one said to the other. "Yous lot are always doing good things round ere'. It might not have been much, but it was a little offering of God's joyful, peaceful, whole, generous, peace-filled kingdom at the bottom of Watney Market one Saturday morning.

At Street Level

Rachel Spence, Levenshulme, Manchester

In Romania an item is put outside the house and anyone is welcome to take the item for themselves. It's recycling and reusing at its best. However in Levenshulme, 'what's mine is mine' is the rule to live by, so if someone places an item out the front of their house, within their front yard, it most certainly still belongs to them. With an increase of Romanians living in our street I have found myself on several occasions standing up for the justice element of the Urban Expression value. There will not be peace between ethnic groups until they understand each other's assumptions. I assume if it's in my front yard it's still mine; 'Suspect'(name he gives himself) assumes he can help himself to it. When he does so my neighbours see and build in their minds a negative image of *all Romanians*. When I notice the item has gone I feel hurt and betrayed, for who does not know this unwritten rule? Surely in our conversations with our neighbours it is our duty to explain to newcomers this rule, else how would they know? There is much work to be done, many conversations to be had, a learning curve for all.

How will humans flourish? If they are given space to be themselves, skills to understand others and appropriate interaction together. On *CBeebies* there is a programme called *Little Human Planet*, the theme song says 'Our lives may be so different; Different country, different name; Different language, different weather; But inside we're just the same.' As adults do we lose that belief? And how quick are we to mar our children's beliefs and trust in others?

Then we have our Asian neighbours, desperately seeking to be obedient to Allah, but struggling to watch the injustice of what they see as stealing from people's front yards. But Allah says we must not speak badly of these people but rather if their need is such we should allow them to take. How do we mediate between people for a better neighbourhood atmosphere? And who should be doing that mediation? How are the practicalities brought forth to engage a true demographic of an area?

'It takes a village to raise a child' – well in our inner urban area it takes a community to teach each other the values and unwritten rules of what is acceptable and what is not. 'Oh master grant that I may never seek, so much to be consoled as to console, to be understood as to understand, to be loved as to love with all my soul.' Make me a channel of your peace: it seems to me that neighbourhoods have a responsibility to converse, learn and grow together; this will nurture the vision of *'justice, peace and human flourishing for the city and all its inhabitants.'*

Nick Coke, Stepney, London

I'm sitting around the table with eighteen other people. As it turns out, it's probably the most diverse group I've ever sat with. If I start to think about it, there's so much difference in the room that my head starts to hurt: faith, culture, economics, ethnicity, class, age, education, gender – I could go on. If you pushed me though, I could tell you everybody's name, what's brought them to the table and why they care passionately about a vision of justice, peace and human flourishing for the city. I've spent time with each of them, one-to-one – sitting, sharing, listening and drinking coffee. It appears we have a lot in common – despite the obvious differences.

The day in question is shortly before the 2010 General Election and we're sitting in the London Citizen's office in Whitechapel waiting for David Cameron. He's not yet Prime Minister but he has the look of a PM in waiting. He's just spent half-an-hour walking around the Ocean Estate – that's where we and two or three others around the table live. He later declared it 'a failed project of New Labour' – something to do with the New Deal for Communities fiasco. Whilst he's worrying about that, we're more interested in presenting an alternative vision of the city. It's not the one that's usually associated with places like the Ocean Estate. In our vision – eighteen community 'leaders', representing in turn thousands of others, can sit around a table in complete unity and present five clear and democratically agreed solutions for the flourishing of our East London neighbourhoods. Our vision includes a living wage, a scheme for providing safer streets, a way to provide genuinely affordable housing, an alternative to 'locking up' illegal immigrants and a simple solution to exploitative lending. We've spent years working together on this stuff and we reckon it works. And for us this isn't 'policy', this is life – for our families, our friends, our congregations and our neighbours.

I took my place around the table that day because long ago I realised that as a Jesus-follower, committed to the radical values of the 'upside down kingdom', I could not and would not subscribe to the narrative of a fragmented, broken Britain in our cities. Being committed to a vision of justice, peace and human flourishing for the whole city involves crossing boundaries, building relationships with those not like you, dreaming together and ultimately taking action as partners. In order to bring about genuine change in our communities we need to share the task – we cannot hope to do it alone. My experience has been that in doing so all powers of hell and earth have tried to stop us – and goodness knows it has been hard work at times. But it's been worth it – for the friends I've made along the way, for the genuine outcomes for people in my neighbourhood and church, for the sheer adventure of it all, and for the discovery of God's grace in places I just didn't expect to find it.

Arthur Brown, formerly in Shadwell, London

My years as a member of an Urban Expression Team in East London caused me to reflect many times on the meaning of terms like justice, peace and human flourishing. Often I struggled to see how they were being experienced by those we lived in the midst of. When I looked into the faces of the parents of a crack-addict who had become a close friend of ours, I wondered how they could experience peace, let alone human flourishing in the midst of their pain. At times our 'visions' for these kingdom values just seemed so far off.

And yet a vision cannot simply be something hoped for, sometime in the future. It is something that needs to be lived out, embodied and demonstrated in the midst of conflicting realities.

The thing I like about this commitment is the fact that all aspects are related to the way we relate to each-other and to God. At the heart of a Biblical understanding of justice, be it economic, social or judicial, is the restoration of relationships… relationships between those who have been responsible for injustice and those who have experienced it… the victims and the perpetuators.

These relationships take place within a social context that is typically biased towards the wealthy, powerful and dominant 'few'. As such, any commitment to those who have experienced injustice, or the results of unjust systems, will, in all likelihood, appear to confront those in privileged positions. We need to become part of the process of creating a context in which people's voices may be heard. As a result they are better able to speak up against the injustices that they have experienced which lead to their lack of human flourishing.

A passage that springs to mind is Matthew 21:12-17 when Jesus clears the temple. Essentially he clears one load of 'sinners' out, simply to let another load in. Not only does he seek to welcome those who have been excluded, but he rejoices at the voices the children have been given – albeit to the disgust of the religious leaders! They have become significant participants, rather than observers.

I would also suggest that in being among the poor and seeking to develop a more fair and just society, in which all may experience human flourishing, we seek to humanise those who have become oppressors and dominators, who themselves have become less than the people God would have them be.

Peace also can only really be experienced when the relationships we have with ourselves, with others and with God are reconciled and restored. So many people we knew in Shadwell, as elsewhere, were not at peace with themselves. The 'Shadwell Syndrome', as we often referred to it, was all too common. Local people often felt left behind (particularly as surrounding communities experienced regeneration – even gentrification), abandoned and looked down on. This led to a lack of peace and flourishing and a desire to get out. The fact that people were wanting to move in, to be incarnate, often raised eyebrows and begged the question 'why'? And it was this question that we returned to often... and it was this value, with others, that kept us there.

Lord, we know that you intend for us a world filled with shalom,
your gift of complete well-being to all people,
the whole of humanity,
all who you've created in your image,
who hold holiness and hope
and love and laughter
and peace and purpose
and justice and joy
deep inside their hearts.
But we see too much of lives held down
by systems and sin,
oppression and hate,
domination and darkness,
and we are angry!

So much potential!

Jesus you hold us in your prayer;
you know what life could be for us;
you see how things could change;
you move to drench us in your
transforming love and life.

Help us to see the
possibilities and purposes
in the most broken
of people and places.
Help us to feel your
justice and peace
and your
shalom-filled
creation.

Lord, in your mercy
Let your kingdom come!

 **We are committed to uncluttered church, focused on mission, rooted in local culture and equipping all to develop and use their God-given gifts.**

One of the things that draws many people into church planting or involvement in parachurch organisations, I believe, is a desire to get away from all that stuff in church life which seems to take up so much time but which is intrinsically of little importance. Mike Frost, in his book *Exiles*[9], talks of the yearning many followers of Jesus have for 'communitas' – a deep sense of being in something together, something with a purpose beyond itself, an adventure. He suggests that, having returned from something like a short-term mission trip, many young adults return to their local congregation and experience deep sadness, confusion and frustration about why local congregational life does not seem to embody the same life-giving characteristics as their mission trip. Instead of feeling focused, purposeful and useful, they often feel like there is no clear identity, little motivation and unless people can sing, play an instrument or teach children, their skills are not appreciated or used.

In Urban Expression, whilst we are committed to creating relevant forms of Christian community, many forms of which will indeed require some level of organisation and structure, we do not want to become so cluttered with unimportant stuff that we lose the joy

---

9 Frost.M. *Exiles* (Hendrickson, 2006)

of why we are doing this in the first place. Nor do we want to lose focus on the reason why we feel people will benefit from getting to know and follow Jesus. We hope that we will retain long-term 'communitas'.

In Britain, church frequently seems burdened by imposed structures, some of which we may need to embrace in a considered way, but others which we may need to learn to resist, ensuring that church remains discipled by Jesus rather than by the State and the taxman.

When our team began in 1997 we were free from so many things. We could choose when to meet, how to meet, what to do, it was great! One issue we soon encountered was what to do with our tithes and offerings. We had no bank account and no desire to formalise our finances too quickly, so the easiest option seemed to be to simply collect our money and store it somewhere safe. As we looked around the accommodation we were staying in for somewhere to keep it, we stumbled upon an empty biscuit jar in the shape of a dog! In went our cash and in came a regular 'church' question: 'How much money is in the dog?'

'The dog' proved to be a manageable, simple and useful way to collect and disperse our money, until one day we realised it was perhaps not very sensible to have too large a sum of money in it. Reluctantly some of our team went to open a bank account. In order to keep team life simple we wanted to resist becoming a registered charity for as long as possible, (reclaiming Gift Aid was not as high on our list of priorities as it seems to be on many a church treasurer's!), so we opened a simple club and association bank account with two signatories. We had not yet given our Christian community a name – we had decided early on that we wanted to encourage local people to do this when they started following Jesus themselves. So when asked by the cashier what name to give the account it seemed there was only one option – it was called 'The Dog'. It was simple. It worked well. And it was fun! It helped the finances remain light-hearted and prevented us becoming too serious about it. Our neighbouring team, on opening their bank account, called it the Fridge-Freezer and in their generosity began to support our less financially secure team. So we had the Fridge-Freezer setting up a monthly standing order to The Dog!

Some years later, those who had started to follow Jesus in the neighborhood asked to give the church a name and eventually we took the decision to become a registered charity (for better or for worse!) The time came to close the bank account. With sadness the deed was done. Out of interest the cashier asked, 'Have you stopped racing then?' She had always thought 'the dog' was a greyhound syndicate!

Creating something new can, if managed and supported well, bring a gift of freedom from perceived expectations which dictate how things should develop. The more cross-cultural the context is in which you serve, the more vital it is to be given such freedom to contextualise. We would consider it imperialistic these days to expect an overseas mission team from Britain to impose an essentially Victorian model of church on another culture and yet I would argue that most church planting in Britain is inherently cross-cultural because we are connecting with an increasingly unchurched population, not to mention an increasingly diverse population in terms of ethnicity and faith perspective. In addition there is not one 'urban' culture, but many, so we would never expect the activity of one team to be identical to another and would be disappointed if a team had not given thorough consideration to understanding its context and responding accordingly.

At Street Level

Rich Shorter, Harold Hill

We were leading a parenting course and were talking about how all those attending[10] were good gifts to their local community. We asked them to turn to each other and say 'you are a good gift to our community'. Watching, it was clear people could say it but could not hear it. They struggled to have someone look them in the eye and say they are gifted. Before starting to see people use and develop their God given gifts we've needed to help them see and know that they actually have gifts.

We are still in early days, but I guess our commitment to this value is expressing itself in the following ways.

Listening to each other: in a world which is not great

---

10 The group included fourteen parents referred by social services, many of whose children were on child protection plans

at listening to each other and a place where 'ordinary peoples' voices are drowned out by the professional, we regularly try to have times of sharing and listening to what people think about our community and what they want from it and want it to do. This, we hope, gives people confidence to express themselves and grow in confidence about who they are.

Small steps: we have people who are great on Facebook, excellent cake makers, poster creators and great with kids. Now they have much more to offer than these simple gifts, but they don't have the confidence to yet, and so, when we can, we ask them to use their smaller gifts in the hope that they will one day be able to see how they are already offering and giving to their community.

The bi-product of being committed to help people grow in confidence to use their gifts is the need to be uncluttered. To help people take small steps to grow you need a simple, not complicated and beyond reach way of doing things. You also need to be focused on the local culture and the gifts that dwell there rather than an imported set of expectations about the sort of 'gifts' church and a community needs.

This value is at the core of seeing a healthy local community and church. It is also at the core of having a community which is growing, to understand that it is already full of gifted people who are good gifts to their/our community and so they don't really need us.

Pete Burgess, Stepney

Hope:asha began life nine years ago. The church was

planted by the Salvation Army on the Ocean Estate in the heart of London's East End. Ruth and I joined the church eight years ago as Urban Expression team members. The following are some reflections about what it means to be a church in a missional, urban context.

Gathering

At *Hope:asha* the emphasis is on relationships with each other and this is reflected in how we gather together. On Sundays we eat brunch together before the more formal part of our worship. This is a chance to catch up and share stories. When we have our more formal worship we sit in a circle so we can see each other. There are lots of interactive parts to the worship and people are encouraged to ask questions or make comments.

We also gather to serve the community. *Good Neighbours* happens once a month and gives people linked with the church opportunities to gather together to help others through acts of kindness, such as gardening, cleaning up and decorating. Lots of different people have joined us for *Good Neighbours*. Some are Christian, some are not. Again, working together helps us to build relationships with each other. After the work we eat a meal together. We celebrate what we have achieved together and enjoy each other's company.

Parties have played a big part in the development of our church. We celebrate as often as we can and invite friends in the local community to join us. We have held parties for Christmas, Harvest, Easter, Mother's Day,

Summer Garden party, Guy Fawkes Night and Pancake Day. Again the emphasis is on getting to know each other and meeting new people. Food is a central part of these parties. A friend who visited our church recently said that you could see the strong and deep relationships that people have with each other. I think one of the reasons these relationships flourish is through how we gather together.

Eating

A theme that runs through all the different types of gathering is food. We have found that eating together and developing relationships and community seem to go hand in hand. At parties it seems to be easier to approach people I haven't met before when we are queuing at the food table. We can discuss what is on offer and what looks healthy, tasty or fattening! There is something about eating together that helps people relax. I remember meeting Sarah for the first time at a church party. Whilst we ate together she shared a lot of her life story with me but was also keen to emphasise that she was not into organised religion. She has become a close friend and valued member of our church. She would probably still say she is not into organised religion, but values the relationships she has found through being part of the church. For some people we meet, eating together also has a very functional purpose. Friends who are homeless or have difficult lives may join us to eat out of necessity.

Belonging

When Ruth and I joined *Hope:asha* the church was made up of six adults and two children. Lots of people have come to the church in the last eight years. Some have come along and stayed for a while, others have passed through, some have made it their spiritual home. One of the joys of the church for me was the people who wanted to stay with us. Often they were people with no church background or a nominal Catholic background. Sometimes people with chaotic lives chose to join us, people who struggle with addiction or mental health issues. What I love about *Hope:asha* is that because we emphasise community and relationships in the way we gather, people can feel part of the church regardless of their faith or lack of it. It is through these relationships we can help each other to meet with Christ.

Sometimes it is hard to answer the question "How many people come to your church?" We have relationships with many people, some come to Brunch Church, others come to *Good Neighbours* or the parties, some come to other activities. Some used to come to things but don't now, yet we still have relationships with them. How do we decide who is part of the church community, who is in and who is out? Maybe 'How many people come to your church' is the wrong question. Maybe the question should be 'How many people do you know, how many people do you have relationships with?'

Jesus, preserve us from the trappings of church life,
    from endless discussions
        about things that have no weight
            or relevance in your kingdom.

Jesus, protect us from distractions and trinkets
                that blur your vision in us.
Jesus, deepen in us a love for the rhythms that surround us;
the cultural joys of our streets
        and parks
            and homes
                and places of refuge.
Raise up among us
    men and women
        young people and children
            with the gifts needed to build your
                kingdom here.

Give us the sight to spot the gifts already here that need
to be encouraged,
and given oxygen,
      light,
          compost
                – whatever it takes for these gifts
                    to grow!
Make us muck-loving gardeners in your kingdom!

Lord, in your mercy
Let your kingdom come!

 We are committed to unconditional service, holistic ministry, bold proclamation, prioritising the poor and being a voice for the voiceless.

'Do you love people because you want them to become Christians, or do you want people to become Christians because you love them?' I remember how dumbstruck I felt when I first heard this poignant question asked by the Anglican evangelist, David Watson. It was one of many thought-provoking issues Stuart Murray Williams would raise with his church planting students at Spurgeon's College, of which I was one back in the mid-90s.

The issue of social action has bleeped with different levels of urgency on the radar of the church in Britain throughout history and notably often feels less important for those facing the least social needs. When writing the values it seemed obvious to my husband Jim and me, having already served almost a decade in the inner city, that holistic service to people in poverty was a non-negotiable. Whether people want to explore faith or not, our calling as followers of Jesus is to model God's love in any ways we can. This is especially true when serving those who are most marginalised or feel least noticed or heard.

In reporting their investigations into the causes of the UK riots in the summer of 2011, *The Guardian* and *The London School of Economics* proposed that one key aspect was those on the margins feeling like they were not being heard[11]. Whether unemployed young people with lack of aspirations, members of Black or Ethnic minority communities who feel repeatedly mistreated by the police, or members of the Occupy movement who felt the public were paying for the bankers' bonuses, their commonality was that they felt their voice did not count. Martin Luther King is often attributed to have said that riots are the voice of the unheard, and part of our role in a holisitic approach to mission needs to be reassuring those who feel voiceless that they are indeed heard and valued.

It is easy, when living in an inner-city community, to still prioritise those we feel most comfortable with. If we feel most comfortable with those with a certain education, income or accent we can live in an urban community but effectively be disengaged from some parts of it. There are many who live in challenging areas of our cities who effectively commute between friends with no awareness of their neighbours. The call to prioritise the poor encourages Urban Expression teams to make serving the poor a core element of what we are about rather than an optional extra, to have eyes that are open and ears that are tuned in to this priority at all times.

11 Reading The Riots online report,
http://www.guardian.co.uk/uk/interactive/2011/dec/14/reading-the-riots-investigating-england-s-summer-of-disorder-full-report, accessed 08.27 17.07.12
Further Reading The Riots research articles:
http://www.guardian.co.uk/uk/series/reading-the-riots accessed 08.27, 17.07.12

What bold proclamation looks like in a marginalised community which has had mission 'done to' it by many a short-term visitor remains a challenge for many of us. I do not doubt any of our team members' desire to communicate effectively the story of Jesus and its transformative potential, but many of us have struggled to know how to do that in ways that do not feel cringey, judgmental and unrelational. The use of art, story, party and other relational activities have usually been the most effective. I really like Chris Duffett and Simon Goddard's book *Big Hearted*[12] which gives examples of many bold, creative, thought-provoking and yet fun ways of proclaiming the Gospel, some of which could translate well into urban contexts. What we have experienced is that bold proclamation is received best in the context of relationship, so perhaps the more we grow to love someone, the more we might want them to know the power of the Jesus story in the reality of their lives too.

At Street Level

Sharon Jones, formerly in Shadwell, London

I've always been someone who likes to be different, to break out of the mould, to look for new ways to be and do. So fitting into Urban Expression wasn't too difficult! It was 1999 and I wanted to be in the inner city, making meaning out of struggle and finding joy in the concrete

---

12 Duffett.C. and Goddard.S. *Big Hearted* (Gilead, 2012)

jungle. With God's divine plan in full swing, I ended up living next door to Jim and Juliet Kilpin as I moved to the 'East End' to train as a primary school teacher.

I intentionally chose to be alongside those on the margins and it surprised many. 'Oh you're so brave,' they'd say, 'living in Shadwell'. A colleague once told me it was the scariest place they'd been to in London; but when somewhere is your home, it brings with it a sense of belonging and peace (though I must confess that I inevitably got scared a few times!).

This desire to be rooted in the reject pile of desirable living locations was resonated in the value 'we challenge the trend of some Christians moving out of the cities and encourage Christians to relocate to the inner cities.' In fact I experienced God's incredible provision of £30,000 to put down the deposit on a flat! It demonstrated to the community my commitment to being there, which was especially powerful given that many of the locals wanted to move out of, rather than in to, the local estates.

I believe my biggest failing was not being bold enough in my proclamation of the gospel as expressed in one of the values. 'We are committed to unconditional service, holistic ministry, bold proclamation, prioritising the poor and being a voice for the voiceless.'

I appreciated greatly the relationship-building focus we had, and did understand the 'belong, believe, behave' viewpoint we took. However, on reflection, my fear of damaging friendships held me back from being more direct about the truth they needed to hear. Sadly, although I may have been a link in the chain, I didn't directly help bring one person to faith in Jesus in six years.

Why not? It was a personal weakness, but maybe also in those early stages we were so focused on 'being' and helping people to belong, that we didn't equip ourselves to fight more urgently for the saving of lives and cleansing of sin. Because the only kind of 'life-giving relationships' that we need to be building are the ones where people choose to have Christ as their Lord. He is 'the way and the truth and the life' (John14:6). 'Because we loved you so much, we were delighted to share with you not only the gospel of God but our lives as well' (1 Thessalonians 2:8). The two have to go together; you can't share your life without sharing the gospel.

I must also say, as I look back, that I never fully got to grips with understanding the local culture. I made plenty of mistakes and there are many things I'd do differently now. But the security that you find when you are allowed to try, fail and try again, is liberating. I loved that about our team. I find it an unusual and necessary value of Urban Expression. 'We recognise the importance of taking risks and the demands of mission in the inner city, and we believe that it is acceptable to fail.'

Creativity is about experimenting. Not everything worked out how we thought it would, or something had a season and then it was time to move on. I found it challenging to maintain flexibility and responsiveness to local needs but it is something that is vital to urban ministry. I hold onto this idea, and many other things I learnt during my special time with what was Cable Street Community Church. They still influence me now I'm involved in urban ministry in poor areas of Lima, Peru.

Paul Ede, Possilpark, Glasgow

How do Spirit-led missional connections begin to form? How do we engage in 'pattern recognition'[13] in the midst of a complex missional environment? The foundational skill is listening. In Acts 10, Peter submits himself to listen carefully in at least three different contexts: listening to God (10:9-16, 19, 47), listening to the community (10:22-23a; 25-33) and listening to the church (10:23b).

Peter also practises the giving and receiving of hospitality. He gives hospitality to the men of Cornelius and submits himself to the hospitality of their gentile master. Hospitality here creates space for encountering the other and discovering the Spirit's revelation of the gospel. Hospitality facilitates reconciliation. Perhaps this is one reason why Peter is so keen to encourage the early Christians to 'offer hospitality to one another without grumbling'[14].

My own experience in Possil has led to reflection on the limits frequently set on the dynamics of hospitable listening. It has certainly been the case that discovering, befriending and listening to those who have power within and without the immediate relational networks of Possil has helped me recognise patterns and connections in the spiritual and relational map of our host community. In this way it was possible, for example, to hear the convictions of our local Green

13 Cray.G. *Discerning Leadership*. (Grove Books, 2010) p24
14 1 Peter 4:7

councillor as to the need for environmental change. And yet in our context it has been just as critical, if not more so, to engage in hospitable listening with those have no power. Scripture constantly reminds us that God listens to the cry of the poor, often over and against those who hold power (Job 34:24-28).

Guided by the Urban Expression value of being a 'voice for the voiceless,' it has proved essential and richly rewarding to first emulate God and listen to those voices, dignifying and allowing them to change us, before presuming to speak on their behalf. An example of this would be spending time with the local mother who founded *To Play or Not to Play*[15], a grass-roots charity dedicated to environmental improvements on behalf of kids, hearing her concerns, and in so doing building a foundational friendship for our ongoing work together.

But does even this exhaust the limits of hospitable listening? During the initial listening phase of the church-plant, I would commonly go on prayer-walks around Possil, exploring the fringes of the community and deliberately seeking out the nooks, crannies and hidden passage-ways that would have become familiar to me had I grown up in Possil. It was hard to avoid the amount of derelict and vacant land that blights our community – it hits your face as soon as you step out the door. I have since discovered that everyone in Possilpark lives within 500 metres of a derelict plot of land. This

---

15 *To Play or Not to Play* (Online: http://www.toplayornottoplay.org.uk/ – accessed 24-12-11)

compares to a Glasgow-wide average of 60.3%, and a Scotland-wide average of 29.8%. This constitutes a significant environmental injustice.

But it was also during one such walkabout that I stumbled upon the Clay Pit for the first time – an area of twelve acres just a mile north of the city centre and just at the edge of our community which has since been described by the conservation officer of the Christian Environmental charity, A Rocha, as an 'ecological goldmine'.

As I wandered through the varied terrain, discovering the beauty of the canal at its edge, the signs of urban neglect, and especially the awesome panorama it affords of the city of Glasgow, it became increasingly clear that this was a special, but under-utilised spot. And yet it was just as clear that it needed care and attention to fully express God's intended glory. I believe that through the Spirit I heard both the groans and the praises of creation that day (not just the groans of the people of Possil):

- 'The heavens declare the glory of God; the skies proclaim the work of his hands. Day after day they pour forth speech; night after night they display knowledge. There is no speech or language where their voice is not heard. Their voice goes out into all the earth, their words to the ends of the world.' [16]
- 'Let the heavens rejoice, let the earth be glad, let the sea resound, and all that is in it; let the fields be jubilant, and everything in them. Then all the trees

---

16 Psalm 19:1-4

of the forest will sing for joy; they will sing before the Lord.'[17]
- 'We know that the whole creation has been groaning as in the pains of childbirth right up to the present time.'[18]

This was a pivotal moment in beginning to explore the possibility that the Spirit was leading the church in the direction of brownfield rehabilitation as mission. I had been welcomed by creation into a haven of hospitality and peace and had listened to creation as given voice by the Spirit.

One member of the church suggested that the Urban Expression value of being a 'voice for the voiceless' must also count for creation, when its voice is suppressed through disregard, neglect or exploitation. Sallie McFague suggests that in our contemporary context with regards to the biblical call to extend reconciliation to the marginalised other, 'the earth is the new poor.'[19]

Anglican Bishop Graham Cray writes that 'discernment involves a triple listening – to God directly, to the Christian community or team you lead, and to the local community or relevant network to which you are called.'[20] But in light of our contemporary context, could it be that we need to discover a fourth dimension: that of listening to the Spirit speak through non-human

17 Psalm 96:11-13
18 Romans 8:22
19 McFague S, *Super, Natural Christians: How We Should Love Nature* (London: SCM, 1997)
20 Cray, G. *Discerning Leadership* (Grove Books, 2010) p18

creation? Should we not also listen to the groans of creation (Rom. 8), not just the community to which we belong, the church of which we are a part and, of course, the God who is our Lord? If the Spirit is that same Spirit that is drawing all of creation into reconciliation with the Father through the Cross of Christ, and creation is capable of both singing God's praises and groaning in distress, then the missional leader also needs to be able to listen to the voice of creation, so often rendered voiceless in the culture of Modernity. By listening to this voice to the voiceless, the Urban Expression Possil team (now Clay Community Church)[21] has been led into a fascinating new practice of urban eco-mission.

---

21 www.claychurch.org.uk

Lord you have given us everything.
There is nothing we have
that doesn't come from you,
a holy gift of divine grace.
You gave us your life
and every breath that we breathe reminds us of that.

We come to you in humility and hope
offering ourselves to you again knowing our own frailty.
You know the demons that lurk within us
of weaknesses and compulsions,
addictions and obsessions;
of lack of confidence
and self-limitations.

Lord, you are much more generous
to us than we are to ourselves
and you see us for who we are,
with our confused motives
and clashing hopes and fears.

But we want to be your people here
who point to your coming kingdom
and your sacrificial love.
So in our fragility
        take us,
            make us,
                and use us.
                    We are yours.

Lord, in your mercy
Let your kingdom come!

 **We are committed to respecting and building relationship with other faith communities and averse to all forms of manipulation or erosion of liberty.**

The Anabaptist movement grew in a time when there was no religious liberty. Less than five hundred years ago it was punishable to not go to church, not pay taxes to the church and not have your children baptised.

That might seem a long time ago and may bear little resemblance to twenty-first century Britain, yet the ripples of an all-powerful 'Christendom' still warp the reflection of God's church and disturb the surface of mission. Some lament the declining influence of 'the church' in Britain and wish we had power to make things 'Christian' again. Many Christians get confused when our government appears to side with those of other faiths or none, and this often provokes backlash from the Christian community and the Christian-leaning media.

Whilst Jesus followers might be concerned about the values undergirding our society and the potential of individualism, consumerism and selfishness to pull our nation apart, we have to be careful that our underlying responses do not unwittingly suggest it would be better if we could force everyone to behave in Christian ways. The truth is that many people of other faiths and of none share our concern for the well-being of society and there is much we can collaborate on. If we truly desire transformation for our most deprived communities it makes sense that we work together. Of course, if we are only concerned about how many people 'come to church' this won't be a priority for us, but if we have a kingdom, shalom, holistic outlook, this will be high on our agenda.

Even in our more recent mission history there are shocking stories of bribery and coercion – practical help sometimes only being offered to those in intense poverty on condition that they come to church or a Bible study. Whilst the motives might be of genuine desire for people to encounter the Christ who gave his life for them, this approach walks a dangerous line which in a multi-cultural, multi-faith context seems more and more unacceptable. Finding genuine ways to walk with and learn from the 'other' (explored brilliantly in Kester Brewin's book of the same title[22]) in the hope that authentic dialogue might take place seems paramount and something many of the Urban Expression teams, I am pleased to say, have taken seriously.

At Street Level

Kerry Coke, Stepney, London

Since the day we arrived in Stepney, my role in crossing the divide between ourselves and those of a different faith has been centred on women. In an attempt to meet local people when we first arrived I went along, as a mother with small children, to parent and toddler

---

22 Brewin,K. *Other* (Hodder & Stoughton, 2011)

groups, where I was the only non-Muslim in the group. This quickly led to me being known and accepted, and I was given the opportunity to go into Bengali women's homes, as they were invited into mine! I was surprised at how curious they were, particularly at Christmas time, to see what a real Christmas tree looked and felt like, and to discover that they wouldn't get a bad jinn from being in the home of a Christian.

When my children started school, I was really saddened to see that the parents would stand in groups according to which ethnic culture they were. So, in the playground there would be groups of Bengali mums standing looking inwards, groups of Somali mums doing the same, a group of white middle class mums in a closed circle and a group of white working class mums not even feeling able to come in through the gates!

I wanted to do something about this self-separation, so I started to stand in the 'wrong' part of the playground and just started chatting to the Bengali mums. I felt confident doing this because of the years of experience when my children were younger. Quite quickly I was accepted and was able to introduce mums of different backgrounds to each other. But I wanted to push it a bit further…

I spoke to the Headteacher about starting a friendship group at the school. She was really excited about the idea, so initially we gathered at the school or in a local cafe straight after dropping the children off on a Friday morning. But I wanted to push it a bit further…

I felt that what I wanted to create was a friendship group which met in each other's homes, allowing

English mums the chance to see what it looks like in the home of a Bengali Muslim woman, and vice versa. Because I had spent time building a network of women around me, it wasn't difficult to make the leap from meeting in a community environment to meeting in a personal, home environment. The ongoing results from this very simple idea have been extraordinary. The group meets every week without fail, with different women offering to open up their home to others. Dozens of women and their families have been touched by this act of open, honest friendship. We are able to ask questions about each other's faith and lifestyle in a non-threatening kind of way. It's not unusual for the woman hosting the group to invite other family members along to 'come and see'!

And the beautiful thing about this group is that everyone knows it is special – I have even heard it referred to as sacred. There are two moments I can think of particularly when it was very evident that the kingdom of God had broken in. The first was when we were leaving the home of a Jewish woman, having been a group made up of Christian, Muslim, Atheist, Zoroastrian, Agnostic, Secularist and Jewish women. We had spent the morning together and as we stood outside her house, there was a moment when we just hugged each other – some with tears rolling down their faces – when we knew that what we had created was counter-cultural. From my perspective, the presence of God was very powerful at that moment.

The other key moment happened last year at Sunbury Court. I was able to bring a group of twelve women from within this friendship group away for the weekend. The aim was to really get to know each other and have a bit of fun at the same time! During the Sunday we were treating ourselves to a bit of pampering using the skills that we had in the group – massage, make-up, nails, that kind of thing. As you can imagine, a group of twelve women make a lot of noise with our constant chatter, but there came a moment when silence fell for a minute or two and we just looked at each other and smiled as we realised we had grown comfortable enough with each other to be still. And I knew the reality of the song 'Be still, for the presence of the Lord the holy one is here'. I never fail to be surprised at where God turns up!

Tom and Barbara Ward, Forest Gate, London

The Holy Habit of Hospitality

A three hundred year old proverb says; 'An Englishman's home is his castle'. Many Christians act as if this is a good idea. They keep people out. The Word of God is clear we are to practise hospitality. Jesus practised hospitality not only to his disciples but to others. Since Jesus expected his disciples to receive hospitality from non-believers, people of peace, it is no surprise that we are expected do the same for others.

What is hospitality? Literally it means showing love to strangers. It is sharing what you have with others—not worrying about what you don't have. It is having an open door to your home. It is welcoming not just your friends, or those who you are familiar with but also those who are different. It is not behaving as if 'your home is your castle' and shutting others out so you can protect your privacy. The early church met in homes and Paul taught from house to house.

Jesus often received hospitality from others and one time Jesus corrected the religious leader who did not show common cultural courtesies of hospitality. We are commanded to gather together even more as the end draws near, encouraging each other to love and do good deeds—what better place to gather together than in one another's homes. Peter says the end of all things is near—Christ is coming back—what should we be doing? Offering hospitality!

We, who have chosen to return to the city, live with the disadvantaged, the vulnerable, those on the fringes of society, need to ask: 'Are we being good stewards of the things God has entrusted to us?' Many of the nations that have come to the UK (there are over three hundred languages spoken in London – one in eight being Muslim) highly value hospitality. We need to open our homes and our hearts – being family to those who are alienated from many or most of their loved ones. If the church of the 21st century is going to be relevant it will not come from copying the norms of the 21st century – especially as they relate to the use of our wealth and homes. We must be radically different and love people Biblically – by sharing with our words and our wealth.

The Urban Expression church plant in Forest Gate has used hospitality to build bridges and as the primary vehicle for growth of its members. Hospitality can be very simple, such as inviting people over for a cup of tea or watching a movie together, to serving a big meal, to having people during holiday times (Christmas, Easter etc.) or even opening your home for people to stay overnight or longer. Not only have Buddhists, Hindus, Muslims and Sikhs been the recipients of hospitality, but Anglo and African-Caribbean Englishmen have shared with the blessing of receiving and giving hospitality. We have seen people hardened by life and religion soften over a cup of tea, we have had people share a meal and then pray to receive Christ.

As God shares and blesses us through others we want to be good stewards and used of God to bless others with the hope that people's faith will be built up and many will become faithful, fruitful followers of Jesus, practising the holy habit of hospitality.

Jesus you have placed us in a place of such difference!
We offer to you our neighbours,
Muslim, Hindu, Sikh,
Jew, Buddhist,
and those of confused faith
or no faith at all.

Help us to see you in their eyes,
celebrate you in our relating,
embrace new truths of you
that we learn in our common life,
and may our words and actions
be filled with gentleness and respect.

You call us to be a people of dissent
where prevailing culture and ways
deny a voice to the voiceless;
and we pray for strength and courage
to speak out and act up
when basic human rights are trampled on.
And in so doing, help us to address
the manipulative tendencies in our
own hearts that damage others
and limit ourselves.

You are Lord!
And we will live in freedom!
Alleluia! Alleluia!

Lord, in your mercy
Let your kingdom come!

Core Values – Humility

 We acknowledge our dependence on God and affirm our continual need of prayer and God's empowering Spirit.

In the inner city your senses are bombarded with the beauty of diversity and creativity, but also with challenge. Most issues faced in urban communities are not unique to cities, but it is often the density, the concentration of issues, that can feel quite overwhelming, and this is what makes urban mission distinctive.

Knowing you are moving into a neighbourhood which has been marginalised or stigmatised for decades, if not centuries, causes you to ask why such challenges have remained for such a long time. It also causes you to consider how effective you are likely to be at bringing about substantial transformation.

Those who have been committed to urban mission for the long haul are often dubious about new 'do-gooders' moving into a neighbourhood. They come with their ideas, their visions and sexy strategies, but long-termers know how draining and exhausting the reality is and whilst they do not wish for failure, they may find themselves waiting to see how committed the newcomers really are. I remember seeing a church leader from another part of Tower Hamlets six or seven years after we moved to Shadwell. He was not someone we saw regularly and so we had only followed each other's stories from a distance, but his encouragement indicated something of his expectations. 'Well,' he said, 'you're still here. Well done!'

In such contexts it is vital to acknowledge our dependence on God. People have tried for decades to bring positive change to some places. Some have struggled, some have moved on, some have burnt out. Yet some, by the grace, strength and patience of God and with learnt skills of understanding, contextualisation and tenacity, have managed to stay long-term and experience significant change in their own lives and those they have lived amongst. There is no reason why Urban Expression teams who intentionally acknowledge their dependence on God and find meaningful ways to be empowered by the Spirit might not experience the same.

At Street Level

Tim Presswood, Openshaw, Manchester

Higgs Boson Particle Accelerator

How do I begin to describe this prayer? It was the Sunday after the Higgs Boson Particle Accelerator had been successfully turned on. I am not a scientist, I do not know if there is such a thing as a God particle, but this is a wondering prayer that attempts to reflect on a major scientific event in the context of our worship.

Dear Particle,

I feel a bit daft, praying to something smaller than the smallest speck of dust, but the newspapers call you the 'God particle,' so I suppose I had better get used to it!

You were certainly there, a long time before me. You were there a long time before human beings. Or cave dwellers. Or dinosaurs.

You were there before the earth grew, fragmenting off the sun, trapped in its gravitational orbit.

You were there before the solar system exploded into being, and before the universe stretched out its carpet of beautiful stars.

In that blink of the eye, when the first matter exploded into being, when the big bang – which can't have been very big actually because particles are so small – when the big bang cracked, you were there bringing mass into being.

So dear particle…

Perhaps soon we will find you, observe you. Perhaps one day, we'll be able to answer the questions about how you brought this wonderful world into being.

But not why.

There are so many questions which science cannot answer.

A particle cannot explain why the universe exists.

A particle cannot explain love.

Or hate
Or generosity
A particle can be beautiful
but it cannot speak of why beauty exists.

Why would a man willingly die for someone he hadn't met?

That is beautiful
and stupid.

It makes no sense.

It serves no practical purpose.

Perhaps you haven't taken away all the mystery of the universe.

Perhaps we should keep on praying together...

© *Clare McBeath & Tim Presswood*

Angie Tunstall, Eccles, Manchester

Picture a child on a swing. The swing is pushed out... it comes back, it goes out, it comes back, out... back, out... back... A familiar rhythm that can also offer us a pattern for prayer.

Early in his story Mark shows us Jesus' dependency on his Father and his continual need of prayer and God's empowering spirit (Mark 1:14-38). At the end of a hard day's work in the synagogue, Jesus and his friends set out to chill with a weekly Sabbath meal. The interruptions begin, as Simon's mother-in-law is sick with a fever and Jesus heals her. The locals arrive with the demon possessed and the sick and the interruptions continue. In urban life often the demands don't stop, they just keep coming: week in, week out, in the workplace, in the community, in the family, in the home.

It's very early in the morning and Jesus seeks to find a solitary place – a place of solitude. It was his regular pattern, a habit of his heart, to go away from the crowds and spend time *being* with his Father: conversing *with*, communing *with*, listening *to* his Father. A place to redress the imbalances of life, to be restored. A place of dependency and to discern the will of his father.

Look closely and we see the pattern emerging: deep engagement with the needs of humanity, followed by withdrawal from the demands, and deep engagement with the Father. Engagement... withdrawal, out... back, out, back... engagement with life's joys and celebrations, exposure to the fragmentation and brokenness of the evils and injustices that confront on a daily basis. Withdrawal as God speaks and restores our spirit and times to discern and know God's will for the next stage of the journey – the next day, week, month etc.

Ignatius of Loyola believed that God deals directly with people, and God's dealing makes a difference. In Mark's story, after Jesus spent time with the Father, he was able to resist the demands of the people around him setting the agenda and was able to say, 'we need to go somewhere else... '

Ignatius also developed the practise of Examen[23], encouraging us to begin prayer by considering how God is looking at us, as God always desires to spend time with us, enabling us to come with a sense of expectancy, followed by moments of gratitude. Dependency

---

23 For more on Examen see www.ignatianspirituality.com

involves asking God for insight, and for Ignatius this is discerned by reviewing our day (week, month), reflecting on both negative and positive emotions. Surprisingly, this can be the place we discern God's direction and empowering spirit leading us in trust and confidence as Jesus followers.

In urban living, this simple understanding of prayer enables me to live the Urban Expression value of dependence on God, our need of prayer and of God's empowering spirit.

Our brother Jesus
without you we are nothing
we can do nothing
create nothing.

You are the vine
we are the branches.
And you call us your friends
and invite us to dwell in your love.

When life gets busy
and the demands never-ending
we find that hard.
It's hard to be still
and to stop our minds from whirring,
and thinking about the next
thing that needs doing.

But we say again that
we need you
we yearn to be closer to you
we long to deepen our understanding
and our following.

In spite of the noise in our lives
hear the quiet convictions of our hearts and lead us on.

Lord, in your mercy
Let your kingdom come!

 **We believe that all people are loved by God, regardless of age, gender, education, class, ethnicity, sexuality or physical/mental health and that God works through all believers – and others besides.**

There might seem little reason to include this value as most Jesus followers would verbally confess to agreeing with this statement. However, we have found that, although it is easy to say, it is not always so easy to live out in reality, and so an explicit value allows us to regularly ask how we are doing at acknowledging God's love for all. There are inevitably those we feel we can love more naturally and there are always those who push the boundaries of our love and, if we allow them, teach us how to love.

Whilst we might easily say that we love all people, it is interesting to observe how we might treat some differently from others. I remember a story about a dear man called Hugh who got involved in the life of the team and developing church community in Wapping. Hugh had struggled for many years with alcohol and mental health issues. He was well known in the community: some looked out for him, others looked away. One day he turned up at a barbeque organised by this emerging church community which was desperately trying to span the diverse cultures in Wapping – the local, long-term residents and the newly arrived professionals from the recently-built Canary Wharf. The organisers reeled as Hugh extended his hand to shake the hand of one of the gentrified guests only to be rebuffed by a recoiling hand. How painful to watch!

We might also easily say that, of course, God works through all people, yet it still seems to be the educated and most articulate who have most opportunity to see this in practice. To release those who lack confidence or reading skills or personal hygiene or have speech impediments to serve others, to lead others, to speak and nurture others, takes intentional action and patience. It also takes an understanding across the whole community of Jesus followers that this is important; otherwise the required patience and open-heartedness to hear God speak through the other who is not like me, might not be discovered.

Hugh was also a big fan of The Lord's Prayer. Many will remember how at each and every gathering he would ask if proceedings could conclude with The Lord's Prayer. The first few times it was a respected novelty, then it became a bearable annoyance and later, for some, it might have become a predictable distraction from what God was really doing. On one occasion I simply remember sitting in a small group with Hugh with people sharing stories and testimonies. I cannot remember now what the topic was, but I do remember clearly a feeling that, as Hugh asked *again* if we could pray The Lord's Prayer, it felt exactly the right response to the stories that had been shared. There was a moment of sarcastically-raised eyebrows, but the reality of God's Spirit was there. Several of us could sense that this was truly a holy moment, which had been led and initiated by dear Hugh.

This value is probably the one that has caused most diversity of opinion across Urban Expression to date. The idea that God works through all believers and others besides raises questions of God's mission ('Missio Dei') and how to identify what and who God chooses to be involved with and at what level. Can a Muslim teach a Christian something about Jesus? Can an atheist reveal something of God's kingdom? Can a person for whom God is her Mother teach in Sunday School? Can a person who has changed their gender be in leadership of a Christian community? Can a gay partnership be healthier for someone than a string of abusive heterosexual relationships? Can a heroin addict teach a prostitute user about love?

There are no simple answers to these questions, but we have learnt increasingly over the years that Urban Expression teams need to have their eyes open to what God is doing in their neighbourhood, and also have their hearts open to the fact that God might be doing something that looks a little different in another community and that, even though our boundaries are being pushed by each other, we are committed to loving and journeying with one another as we discover more about God.

At Street Level

Sarah Warburton, Stepney, London

A man comes to church. You see an aggressive,

depressed and overweight man. Then you get to know him, his story, his struggles, his faith; and in the meeting he speaks profound truths. Who is the wise, and who is the 'well' person?

A woman you know. She is passionate about God, serving him in difficult situations, speaking out in his name. She then decides to act upon her feelings for another woman. Is her work now worth nothing and is she no longer loved by God?

A Bengali friend notices I am struggling and in her compassion offers to pray for me in the same way that I have offered to pray for her in the past. Will her prayers go unanswered because she is a Muslim?

A teenager sits in the corner of the room, not wanting to be part of the meeting but she has no choice but to be there. She is playing on her phone and is disgruntled. We are writing prayers for a missionary friend abroad. This girl takes the paper and pen given to her and, while we adults get on with writing, she quietly goes out of the room to get her Bible so she can include passages in her prayers. Are we sometimes too quick to judge?

A man of seemingly no faith wants to join our *Helping Hands* project, where once a month we do gardening for people who need help in our area. He says he lives a very selfish life and wants to do something good. Each month he sits with us as we pray, and he joins in with the amen. Is our work that day more important because we do it in the name of Christ, or does heaven rejoice in his selfless act of kindness?

A single mum, whose five children are from three different fathers, struggles with alcohol and depression.

She is on a team of people writing policies for a project the church runs for people with mental health issues. Should the church have waited until she was recovered before putting her in this leadership role?

Before moving to East London the only people I saw serve in the church were those who were 'well', who spoke the 'right' words and had stable marriages. I think the church was poorer because of this.

Jesus came for those who know they have a need for him. He surrounded himself with people who didn't get things right and who struggled with life. Throughout the Bible it is clear that God has a bias to the poor and the marginalised. It is of great sadness to me that people who are on the margins not only feel that they have nothing to offer, but they feel they will not be welcomed in a church and therefore are unloved by God. How can the church have got things so mixed up? Surely the question should be: is there any good news for the rich, the proud and the leaders of our communities?

Holy God
the Bible is filled with stories
of you working through
the unlikely,
the despised,
the stranger,
the enemy,
and you constantly shocked
those who were called your own
and offended their sensibilities.
And for that we thank you!

When we get precious about
who's in and who's out
remind us again of our role models:
Abraham and Sarah, the travelers;
Shiphrah and Puah, the Hebrew midwives;
Ruth and Boaz, the boundary breakers;
Cyrus and Darius, the faithful outsiders;
and all those restored by Jesus
to their full humanity,
and all those in the history of your people
who have defied convention
in subversive ways.

In Jesus you showed us how to love
those who are not like us
but who are adored by you.
Help us to love our neighbours too
and to see you reflected in their faces.

Lord, in your mercy
Let your kingdom come!

 **We respect others working alongside us in the inner city and are grateful for the foundations laid by the many who have gone before us.**

Urban issues are not new. Ever since the first cities the quirky dynamics of a metropolis have been observed, unpacked and engaged with by sociologists, futurologists and urbanologists. But recently the attention paid to cities has increased because urban issues can no longer be claimed to be an optional concern. The United Nations tells us that a tipping point occurred in 2008 and we now live in a world where more people live in cities than don't.[24] The projected figures confirm that this is not a temporary shift but an undisputed trend. Our understanding of, and engagement with, cities is now imperative for global issues of sustainability, particularly in relation to food, fuel, pollution and poverty.[25]

A global movement that believes it has something important to say to the population of the world has no choice but to be concerned about cities. If it is not concerned about cities, it is not concerned about the majority of the human race. And yet you could be forgiven for getting the impression that urban mission

---

[24] For an interactive map detailing the growth visit this BBC News page http://news.bbc.co.uk/1/shared/spl/hi/world/06/urbanisation/html/urbanisation.stm

[25] UNFPA State of The World Population 2007: Unleashing the Potential of Urban Growth
http://www.unfpa.org/swp/2007/english/introduction.html

for Jesus followers is an optional extra, something for those few and far between specialists who have an extra-special calling to such places.

There have indeed been some people who have become significant specialists of urban mission and we in Urban Expression have been privileged to have several such people journey with us over the last fifteen years. We determined at the very beginning not to assume that we knew everything ourselves, but to discipline ourselves to sit at the feet of those with more experience than us, those who have walked the walk and stood the test of time, those who have watched trendy urban projects come and go, but remained behind to pick up the pieces.

We also determined in each locality to be attentive to what had already happened in those places. There are very few places which have not had some form of Gospel witness at some point in their history. The church buildings may be closed now, the theological students moved out to the suburbs, the ethnic church moved with the immigration flow, but there are foundations there which can possibly be built on. There may be sympathies which can be stirred or memories which can be rekindled. Quite often these foundations may have been built by those of a different tradition and it is important that we put misconceptions or presumptions aside and build relationships with those builders so that we can discern whether there are good foundations to build on or not. Often those who have remained in the inner-city are the prayerful brothers and sisters of various religious orders who, in their withdrawal from the world, have actually maintained a long-term holy presence. For the foundations they and others have laid we are grateful.

Sometimes church planters and missional entrepreneurs are put off by the anticipated cold shoulder they will receive from other churches in a community; the 'not in my backyard' mentality. One of the distinctives of urban mission is that generally most Jesus followers are so aware of the acute needs in their neighbourhood that any extra help is well received. When the same level of respect accompanies a preparedness to journey with, and learn from, one another, this help is received even more warmly. Jesus followers who are prepared to do this for the benefit of the Gospel will gain a richness and variety to their work.

At Street Level

Doreen Westley, Newham

As I reflect on this value, the word that strikes me the most is 'respect'. Respect is a word that follows everyone through all walks of life irrespective of status in society; it carries the same weight and meaning whether this is for good or not so good and therefore is very important when working with others.

There is however, a humble challenge when respect is being played out. It may require us to put aside for a time our own agendas in order to explore and embrace our differences and find common ground for dialogue to take place. What will this show of us? Will it portray our humility? Hopefully, yes, knowing that we are not the holders of absolute truth, only God is.

Challenge is always good as it encourages questioning and dialogue with others to stretch our thinking, enabling us at times to re-think and maybe think out of the box. We have to be grateful for this challenge as it enables us to get our foundations secure.

The foundations that have been laid by the forerunners of Urban Expression have left many a legacy, not only in the impact they have had on communities, but also in peoples' lives and the paths and directions they have chosen.

This makes me think back to a number of years ago when hope was born in the hearts of a couple who wanted to make a difference in their community. They grew a church from scratch in partnership with Urban Expression. It only lasted four years. Many might see this as a failure, but the lives of the people that made up this community were very different to one another and each one had been touched by something special God was doing. These people will hold that chapter of their lives forever in their hearts and this has created a strong foundation of hope in what the body of Christ can be. Better to have glimpsed for a short time then never to have glimpsed at all. And because of the community that was formed, individuals still fondly remember the time when they were alive in Christ, they were His hands and feet to the wider community and saw peoples' lives impacted and changed – isn't that what it's about… So let's be grateful for that time.

The word of God states that iron sharpens iron

(Proverbs 27:17): let's not lose sight of the important role respect has as we work together to see His kingdom come and His will be done in our City.

Risen Lord
thank you for the inner city
with its clashing needs and hopes.
It's here that we find you
constantly working to make broken lives whole.
Thank you for calling us to be partners in your work
and thank you for those who work alongside us.

Deepen our friendships;
let our vulnerabilities be shared;
envision us with a fiery passion;
we are your body, one body, and we thank you.

We thank you, too, for all those
who pioneered kingdom building here
.... (fill in names known to you)
who lived prophetic lives
that truly transformed the neighbourhood.

Help us to be like them.
Use us to speak and act prophetically,
and to live lovingly.

Lord, in your mercy
Let your kingdom come!

 **We want to learn from others, seeking to shape what we do in light of the experiences, discoveries, successes and mistakes of fellow-workers.**

Anyone who has spent more than a few years in an urban community will tell stories of their neighbourhood changing. Even in a community where the prevailing outlook is that 'nothing ever happens around here' the tides of urban life ebb and flow all around. Not only do immigration patterns change, but employment levels, relocated companies and businesses, birth rates, buildings opened or closed and the like, all make an impact.

Some optimistic soul once said 'London will be great when it is finished!', but our cities are never completed because in the midst of increasing urban population there is always the need to rebuild the old and create the new. Land is often at a premium in our cities and frequently even on the most unlikely pieces of scrub land a tower block can grow. Conversely, impressive building schemes can unexpectedly grind to a halt leaving communities half knocked-down and neighbourhoods mourning the loss of half their life. Injustice abounds in such instances and some of our teams have experienced the deep sadness and grief of watching a community killed by developers.

Yet change happens, and so we commit ourselves to being on a constant learning journey. A secondary school pupil can expect to have a lesson entitled something like 'Learn to Learn' these days. The principle underlying this concept is that by the time a teenager leaves school, things will have been invented that didn't exist when they entered it. Therefore, an attitude of perpetual learning, rather than one of 'I've learned that already', is essential in everyday life and paramount in an urban setting for a long-term presence.

It is also essential because as Jesus followers we are always learning and discovering more about God, so it is dangerous to say with belligerence that we know the answer to everything because we may well be surprised by God one day. A closed mind and closed heart risks missing the precious revelation of the Spirit that can call us into newness and resurrection of our faith. And as incomplete people who err and make mistakes, it is important that we learn to learn from these with honest reflection, consideration and heaps of grace.

At Street Level

Karen Stallard, formerly in Wapping, London

'Behold, I belong to God like you;
I too have been formed out of the clay.'
(Job 33:6)

'But we have this treasure in jars of clay to show that this all-surpassing power is from God and not from us. We are hard pressed on every side, but not crushed; perplexed, but not in despair; persecuted, but not abandoned; struck down, but not destroyed.'
(2 Corinthians 4:7)

Sustainable ministry can happen when we realise there are others out there trying to do the same job, having the same experiences, discoveries, successes and making the same mistakes. For me this value has been challenging but life-giving as it joins me with my brothers and sisters in Christ with the unity that binds us, the truth that we are all formed out of the clay and that the treasure we have within us is from God. To be able to carry on, remaining full of integrity, we need to know the stories of our sisters and brothers, we need to be able to weep with them and laugh with them, we need to be able to be honest with the disasters and truthful about the shattered hopes.

It is one thing to read the heroic and often romantic tales of 'successful' missionaries who have saved the world and then to feel inadequate, or far worse, to feel the responsibility of saving the world fall on our shoulders. How easily we fall into the omnipotent role-play of being God and forget that we are but clay. However, being able to learn from fellow travelers, to read between the lines of success and hear the tales of failure and brokenness, can give us hope in our hearts as we face the hard reality of life in our work.

If we deny the work of others, if we despise their inadequacies, failings and dodgy doctrine, or if we elevate them into superheroes, then we miss the hidden truths in their stories. The truths which hold the treasure that will keep us going and help us up when we fall.

Working out the above value means listening and allowing ourselves to become fully present as we engage with the stories of past and present workers. Learning how to reflect honestly on their, and our own practice, is crucial. After eight years of working in Tower Hamlets, my practice has changed. I made many mistakes and watched others make mistakes and I have learnt so much through my experiences. I will continue to make mistakes but not all the same ones. I have over the years survived and more than that grown stronger in my own identity and calling, and the stories of others have sustained me and nourished me on the way. I am grateful to my companions, those who I read about in the history books and also those who I have met. They will, I am sure, continue to give me the perspective I need to live a wholesome life along with new friends I meet on the way. I am just like them, made from clay, and just like them I hold a treasure within, which is God.

To summarise, the above value helps us to remind each other of this fact: In our walk with God there is no room for thinking we know the best way, but there is plenty of room for thinking we are not alone on our journey.

Living God
thank you for never leaving us alone
in the work you call us to do.
We thank you for Urban Expression
and everyone who works within it.

Thank you for the richness of experience,
the diversity of gifting,
the depth of hope,
the quality of commitment
all held here.

We pray that our relationships
will be honest, open and true;
that we will never fear vulnerability with each other
but help to build each other up;
through sharing our experiences
reflecting on your presence in them,
discovering who we really are
and working out what we should do.

Help us to listen well to each other
to speak words wisely,
to hold silences sensitively,
to be as willing to learn as to teach ,
so that in all things
you are glorified.
Let your kingdom come!

Lord, in your mercy
Let your kingdom come!

 **We are careful not to drain other local churches of their often limited resources, but hope to be an encouragement and support to them.**

Urban Expression sends teams to 'under-churched' areas of the inner city. This means we are looking for neighbourhoods where followers of Jesus and congregations are sparse. There are some urban areas which actually have quite a strong church presence, often the wealthier or gentrified areas of our cities, or those which have had significant waves of immigration from 'Christian' nations. Such communities are not our top priority because we hope the congregations there may be having an impact already.

It is inevitable, therefore, that any congregations that exist in the neighbourhoods we discern to be under-churched will have a lot on their plate! If they are the only churches for many thousands of people in an area that Jesus followers have avoided, it is likely that the congregations will be small and have probably been faithfully serving God and the community with minimal resources. As such, the last thing we want our teams to do when they arrive is to drain them.

Before a team decides on a locality we encourage the potential team leader or a regional coordinator or steering group to engage in genuine consultation with people in the area. This not only helps to build authentic relationships, but also to discern what strengths the local congregation might have and what the gaps might be that a team could help fill. We feel that it is important for the teams to have freedom to start something new, independent of any existing congregations, but hope that it will complement what is already happening. Whilst there is this freedom to start something new, it is fairly inevitable that partnerships will emerge between teams and existing congregations as well as other organisations, charities or projects in a neighbourhood. I remember when we started in Shadwell we made a decision not to start anything new in the first twelve months but to take time to listen to the community, learn and discern the way forward. We came across a locally-run fledgling youth club which was desperate for help and so the three guys from the team with experience of youth work began to help on a regular basis. This was to prove foundational to many relationships we developed in Shadwell.

We do not want to drain these local groups or congregations of their already limited resources, so we will not seek to poach or entice people to join us. One team, when they arrived in their area, was seen as quite an attractive option to some as they were intentionally focused on a particular ethnic group. Members of that ethnic group who were members of other congregations began to enquire about joining, but in their wisdom the team advised them that they could only join if they were sent by their current congregation as a 'missionary' – to come as helpers rather than consumers of the latest 'thing'. This prevented the team from accumulating too many church-hoppers, which might have distracted them from their main task, but it also ensured that existing congregations were not drained of their resources through a lack of consideration by these new incomers.

Few of our teams have to pay for traditionally burdensome things such as buildings or clergy. One team, as they considered what to do with their 'offerings', decided one Sunday to take a substantial gift round to each of the local congregations in their patch. Imagine the surprise of the ministers as they received cash from the smallest and newest emerging congregation in the area! It is great when you have the freedom and ability to support and encourage others.

At Street Level

Howard Jones, Cobridge, Stoke

When we started with Urban Expression I had been a church minister for twenty-one years. I came into this type of ministry wanting to be free from the often all-consuming job of running the 'church machine' in order to be more available for God and people outside of the church in the local community. However, I am not (and never want to be) one of those 'incarnational types' who almost seem to hate the traditional church. I still love the inherited church and see its value and the enormously important place it has in a community, so I was delighted to find this as one of Urban Expression's key values.

Before we even moved, we made contact with Rod, the local vicar, to reassure him that we were not coming as rivals but as partners. He was very encouraged that

God was bringing more people to Cobridge. When we first moved here it was just the two of us, we knew no one and one of the first places we went was to Christ Church, the local Anglican parish church. The services were much more liturgical than we were used to but we loved meeting the people, and it has opened up all sorts of friendships and ministry opportunities for us.

The three local Anglican churches have a shared community outreach group called 'Pathways', of which Urban Expression Cobridge is now also a partner. This group meets once a month to worship, share stories and pray. One of the main Pathways projects we're involved in is Messy Church, a children's project in another part of Cobridge. We do this with Frank, their community arts worker, who has become a really good friend. Team member Cat and I both have musical gifts which we offer occasionally to the local Anglicans to support them where they have need. I was invited by the curate at St Mark's to be involved in 'Fearless', a monthly worship evening using songs that are slightly more contemporary than the 1980s! St Paul's have no keyboard player so they usually use a backing CD, but they occasionally ask Cat to be a 'live' pianist for a special service. Frank is running a new family service once a month at Christ Church and we support that too.

We know that this relationship is important and it does feel good to be able to help and serve and encourage these local churches. It's not just one way either, it is genuinely comforting to feel part of the wider church in Burslem and not just on our own. One of our most encouraging and faithful volunteers at the ROC Café and the community centre is a wonderful seventy-six year old lady from Christ Church called Margaret. When we told her who we were and why we were here she just beamed and said she'd been praying for this for years. She blesses us in so many ways

In all honesty, it can also be frustrating sometimes. I remember a time recently when Rich and Cat came back from a local church service and just had to spend a bit of time in our kitchen going 'Aaaargh!' Likewise I've been at some local worship evenings thinking 'Howard, what on earth are you doing here?' However, on balance I'm glad we live with this value.

Well, Juliet said we could contribute any way we liked, including poetry. I think Carol Ann Duffy's job is safe, but I thought I'd offer this...

There was a UE team in Stoke
To the local vicar they spoke:
We won't be a drainer
Mate, that's a no brainer
We think you're a jolly good bloke.
We're all in this church lark together
And we all have the same storms to weather
So like sisters and brothers
Let's all help each other
Live now like we hope to for ever.

Living God
your story of our salvation
began with your world's beginning;
and we thank you that you've
invited us to be part of that story today.
Disciples have come before us
and will come after us
and you choose to use us all
in loving the world.

We thank you for brothers and sisters
in other communities around here;
people with hope and vision,
people with questions and concerns,
people searching for truth,
people longing for healing.

In all that we do
keep us attentive to their needs,
their aspirations,
their boundaries
so that we never call from them
something they just can't give
or do
or be
but help us in all our relating
to deepen friendship
and welcome strangers
as we journey on together.

Lord, in your mercy
Let your kingdom come!

 We realise the importance of living uncluttered lives, holding possessions lightly and recognising that all we have is to be at God's disposal.

As well as pursuing uncluttered church, we seek to model this in our lives, recognising that our corporate life as the body of Christ can only ever exaggerate what we are as individuals. Therefore we try to remember that all we have is God's, not just the percentage we offer in sterling, and we encourage one another to be accountable, questioning and good stewards of it all.

Many who have joined Urban Expression teams have shown this in their choices to move into particular neighbourhoods, estates that many residents are looking to move out of rather than move into. They have often chosen to go against the flow of the upwardly mobile and have made decisions which look to an untrained eye to be taking a backwards step. Some team members have given up jobs and taken a risk to find new employment in a new city. Others have given up certain hours in their job so as to be available to the community, considering the gift of time more important than money.

In many teams, although there have not been any that I know of who have chosen a common purse approach, there is a model adopted which encourages open and honest conversation about large purchases. This involves others in the decision making process and reminds us once again that possessions are not ours alone but are God's. Decisions about spending large amounts of money can often be made on a selfish whim;

having the discipline of talking options through with others before drawing a conclusion can be very helpful and can often prevent unnecessary purchases.

Some team members have chosen to live without a car or to car-share, others have loaned money interest-free to enable deposits to be paid for accommodation or mortgages. Several people have supported Urban Expression teams by using their savings to facilitate house purchases rather than have it sit in bank accounts accumulating interest for them alone. Some have shared homes in order to save money, an increasingly popular option in society as a whole as recession bites hard here in Britain.

I am sure there are others who live in community who practise this value at a far deeper level than some of us, and there is much more we can learn, but even at a basic level this value helps us to keep things in perspective and enables us to embark on a journey which embraces risk and rewards us with the wonderful privilege of seeing God provide the things we and others need.

At Street Level

Ellie Morrell, Knowle West, Bristol

What does living uncluttered lives mean? What is it that clutters our path? It might be easy to think of uncluttered as a tidy, minimalist home, or having an efficient, ordered schedule, neither of which reflect much of my home or life, so is there something more to its meaning? Do you ever keep things because you believe one day they might come in useful? Or have you ever had a time when all your well made plans have gone out the window and yet you have experienced a glimpse of 'on earth as it is in heaven' because of the unexpected things that stopped you getting on with your plans? I was wondering: Is there something paradoxical about 'uncluttering' that is about learning to be less efficient in our lives, getting less things done and being less focused on results that enables us to see more of Jesus in our own life and in the lives of those around us? That sometimes it's only by simply being that we see things of great value that we might have otherwise 'decluttered' out of our lives.

Do we choose to walk because we value slowness and face to face human interaction, or is it just quicker to drive? Do we use a dishwasher or do we wash dishes and chat together, because we are not in a hurry to be onto the next thing? We perhaps need to be careful not to focus too much on valuing the speed, efficiency and purposefulness that is often associated with uncluttering and recognise slowness and attentiveness as part of an uncluttered rhythm of life. So in seeking uncluttered lives do we sometimes need to embrace slowness and its inevitable 'less efficient way' so that we can connect with God and discern what is clutter and what is of great value?

As for holding possessions lightly, I'm sure we've all heard lots of teaching on the importance of not storing up material wealth and possessions, but what does this really mean? I wonder if holding possessions lightly is partly about valuing the things that others don't value? I mean, if the burglars are going to break in, they are hardly going to steal the dinner on the stove I spent an hour cooking, or my toddler's cherished artwork, or my husband's gooseberry bush, but to us all these things have a great value because of their meaning to us, not their financial value. Holding possessions lightly is not having the attitude of 'oh well if it breaks I can just go and buy a new one, it wasn't very expensive in the first place', but about cherishing the things you have been entrusted with regardless of financial value. But perhaps more importantly it's about freeing us from material possessions to cherish those priceless things in our lives and the world around us; our celebrations, our faith, our times of sadness, our times of great joy, the sunny day and the seedling carefully planted in faith now growing.

I always love the story of *Jack and the Beanstalk*. Jack sells all his family's worldly possessions for some magic beans and the promise of future riches. He acts in faith and is justly rewarded. I think Jesus would have liked this story and perhaps some of his parables have some of the same elements. Like the parable of the merchant who sells all he has for the priceless pearl and the man who finds treasure buried in the field and sells all to buy the field, there is discernment, faith and action. So may we keep learning that all we have is at God's disposal and to ask God to help remove the clutter of material gain and efficiency from our lives so that we can live wisely and faithfully, continuing to discern and hold close the priceless things of truly great value.

God,
all that we are and all that we have comes from you.
Our possessions, our money,
our breath, our life,
all comes from you.

Where we get tied to stuff
and obsess about acquiring more;
where we fall into thinking
that retail therapy is good for us;
where we find our attitudes
shaped by the advertising we see
rather than the gospel we know
forgive us – and turn us round again
to see the wonder of your gifts,
the generosity of your heart,
the magnitude of your love,
and bring us to our senses!

Preserve us from consumerism;
help us to live more simply;
keep reminding us what you've called us to be;
and in that we will find our joy and our freedom.

Thanks be to God!

Lord, in your mercy
Let your kingdom come!

 We know we are not indispensable and what we attempt to do is part of a much bigger picture, so will try to keep ourselves in perspective.

Change the world. If you don't, someone else will! Urban Expression began with the belief that people can make a difference. It is not only those who hit the headlines, write the books or speak on stages that make a difference, but it is the seemingly insignificant everyday decisions we make that can impact others around us. That money donated to a charity, that word of encouragement spoken, that angry word held back, that forgiveness willingly offered, that invitation given. My own life has taken a dramatically different path to what was projected, all because one family took the initiative to invite a six year old girl to church. Never doubt the impact of small gestures and small beginnings! As Mother Teresa said, 'If you can't feed a hundred people, then feed just one'.

We believe we can make a difference, but we are also acutely aware of how vast the needs of this world are and how tiny a contribution we are able to make. We refuse to allow this to depress or discourage us, but use it to help us gain perspective on our humanness and our place in life. We are part of a much larger story that spans time and space, a story that began before us and will continue after us. We are in the chorus-line of an immense cast, directed by our Creator, working in unison with the others in the line-up. Those with the lead roles have their names in lights only because the wardrobe, technical, sound and prompts are excelling in their roles too. Yet this is not a real-life episode of *The Truman Show* with a script which cannot be deviated from, but a life of choices and values which will disciple us.

This perspective is vital also because our human leaning is to seek value and importance in what we do, that we might feel valued, recognised and needed – indispensable even. Alas the graveyard is full of indispensable people and miraculously the world continues turning as God continues to breathe life into the universe.

Jean Vanier suggests that 'We have to remind ourselves constantly that we are not saviours. We are simply a tiny sign, among thousands of others, that love is possible, that the world is not condemned to a struggle between oppressors and oppressed, that class and racial warfare is not inevitable.'[26] This finite perspective brings freedom to celebrate the bigger story of which we are a privileged part, signposts to the kingdom demonstrating an alternative way of living as friends of Jesus.

At Street Level

Jo Fitzsimmons, Shard End, Birmingham

Sometime when you're feeling important;
Sometime when your ego's in bloom

26 Vanier, J. *Community and Growth* (D.L.T., 1979)

> Sometime when you take it for granted
> You're the best qualified in the room,
> Sometime when you feel that your going
> Would leave an unfillable hole,
> Just follow these simple instructions
> And see how they humble your soul;
> Take a bucket and fill it with water,
> Put your hand in it up to the wrist,
> Pull it out and the hole that's remaining
> Is a measure of how you will be missed.
> You can splash all you wish when you enter,
> You may stir up the water galore,
> But stop and you'll find that in no time
> It looks quite the same as before.
> The moral of this quaint example
> Is do just the best that you can,
> Be proud of yourself but remember,
> There's no indispensable man.[27]

We all need to be needed – it's an emotional need that gives us value and, often, self-worth. As Christian practitioners we are not immune to this. As missional communities we desire to impact our geographical neighbourhoods with radical acts, reflecting gospel truths in our conversations and deeds… without creating dependence, egotistical natures, nor self-aggrandisement.

It is a hard balance: we need to keep ourselves in perspective. We need to take all angles into

---

27 *There Is No Indispensable Man*, Saxon N. White Kessinger ©1959

consideration, humble ourselves to consider every person we have dialogue with, every view point that is held, particularly when it's opposite to our own.

Who do you ask to 'view' you? Whose hands hold you from growing too stale? Whose hands stir up and muddy your waters so you have a different view?
Who tells you that you are a success? Who tells you that you aren't quite hitting the mark? Who's got the perspective right?

God's perspective:

'Do nothing out of selfish ambition or vain conceit. Rather, in humility value others above yourselves, not looking to your own interests but each of you to the interests of the others. In your relationships with one another, have the same mindset as Christ Jesus:

Who, being in very nature God, did not consider equality with God something to be used to his own advantage; rather, he made himself nothing by taking the very nature of a servant, being made in human likeness. And being found in appearance as a man, he humbled himself by becoming obedient to death— even death on a cross!

Therefore God exalted him to the highest place and gave him the name that is above every name, that at the name of Jesus every knee should bow, in heaven and on earth and under the earth, and every tongue acknowledge that Jesus Christ is Lord, to the glory of God the Father.' (Philippians 2:3-11)

Lord,
you've called us to be pioneers
and we have gladly responded
even if some days are hard.
We know that we're looked to
by those searching for more
cutting edge ways of being church
and we carry that responsibility
because we want others to
get the vision.

Sometimes, though,
this adventuring heart
can get a bit full of itself
and we take greater pride
in what we do
rather than who you are.

God save us from
our own self-absorption
our own puffed-upness
and bring us down to earth,
gently if possible.

We know that we are just
a part of your work in the world
and that your Spirit is
healing and transforming
in places we haven't heard of.
But we thank you for this place,
where you've put us now,

knowing that it's as wonderful and valuable to you
as the whole universe.

Thank you God.

Lord, in your mercy
Let your kingdom come!

CORE VALUES – CREATIVITY

 We recognise the importance of taking risks and the demands of mission in the inner city, and we believe that it is acceptable to fail.

This is one of the values which seems to catch most peoples' eye when they first encounter Urban Expression. It is also one of the values which often inspires people to join us. What is it about a group of people that explicitly say they can cope with failure that makes them attractive to join? Surely it would be more attractive to join a group or an organisation which is confident that it will succeed?

Perhaps it is the reason why the value is there that resonates with people? Our reason for including this value is that we believe, as expressed elsewhere, that urban mission is demanding and fraught with challenges. We have enough experience under the belt to know first-hand the rewards and cost of moving into an inner-city estate and do not want to give the impression that teams will be able to move in, adapt to their context, hold down their jobs, maintain their friendships, raise their families, explore relevant ways of communicating the Gospel and developing Christian community and stay sane without some risks along the way! And we prefer to be upfront about this so that people come with appropriate expectations, rather than breeze in and be surprised when it all gets tricky.

Another reason for including this value is that historically there have been very few urban 'church planting' movements that have made a significant long-term impact. Whilst there are a few large churches in our British cities that may appear to buck the trend, the truth is that many inner-city churches struggle, ministers and clergy move frequently, residents move out when opportunity arises, money is in short supply and the glorious chaos of urban life in general sometimes takes its toll. Much interpretation of recent research suggests that those congregations that buck the trend are benefitting from significant immigration from Christianised nations or are focused on university students or the more middle to upper class population[28]. Whilst we give thanks for these trend-bucking expressions of church, the success of small, estate-based expressions of church focused intentionally on the working to lower to under-classes often feels like failure in comparison. Whilst we certainly do not see it as such, we want our teams to be

---

28 Goodhew, D (Ed.), Church Growth In Britain: 1980 To the Present (Ashgate, 2012) Plus helpful articles and summaries - http://religiousintelligence.org/churchnewspaper/?p=26119 and: http://shoredfragments.wordpress.com/2012/06/24/church-growth-in-britain/ Accessed 17.08.12

prepared that onlookers (even well-meaning ones) may well struggle to view their endeavours as particularly successful and they need to be prepared for this cynicism.

So does this value only relate to urban contexts? I would suggest that, as the gap between church and society in Britain becomes increasingly cavernous and we grapple with the effects of secularisation, consumerism, individualism and post-Christendom, Jesus followers need permission to experiment with new ways of connecting with those on the margins. Permission to experiment requires freedom to fail, because it is only in trying something out that we discern if it works or not. Jesus followers in Britain need to resist the safety-obsessed, risk-averse host culture and instead cultivate an environment that endorses trial and error, learning and reflection. After all, if we truly believe that we have a message that can change the world, we will do all we can to train, equip, nurture and release those who can get the message out there and will ensure that we are effectively incubating those experimental, delicate, vulnerable Gospel viruses that might infect those who have not yet been inoculated.

Jean Vanier says 'I am struck by how sharing our weakness and difficulties is more nourishing to others than sharing our qualities and successes'[29], and we hope that our honest story might nourish others who are on a similar experimental adventure too.

29 Vanier, J. *Community and Growth* (D.L.T., 1979)

At Street Level

Paul Stevenson, formerly in Shadwell, London

Picasso is credited with saying 'God is really only another artist. He invented the giraffe, the elephant, and the cat. He has no real style. He just keeps on trying other things.' God keeps 'trying other things', he keeps being creative, talking to us through different things, and like him, we can be creative and talk to each other in different ways too.

The alternative voice that creativity gives to a person is beneficial in two ways. The first is that an idea, viewpoint or feeling can be expressed where maybe conventional methods have failed. For example singing a song outside a bank to campaign against its ethics to stimulate dialogue where petitions and letters may have failed. The second is that the process of speaking it makes the expression more personal and meaningful to the person than if they were to simply tick a box or shake their head in disagreement.

For someone to start speaking in their alternative voice the methods and media to do this need to be accessible. If it is through paint there obviously needs to be paint; if it is through dance there needs to be space. Once the tools are accessible then we can enjoy speaking in our alternative voice, vocalising it in a multitude of ways.

On our estate the council painted our building a colour that they chose. They then gave us an option to decide what colour our doors would be, red, blue or green. But when the doors arrived they were all so dark that you could barely tell them apart. Conventional methods to give us a voice on the new look of our estate had failed. Between the seasons what we found accessible to us was an abundance of flowers and pots that either the shops no longer wanted, or that the council chose to empty their parks and flowerbeds of. Here was an opportunity for all of us on our estate to express ourselves by doing something that was personal and meaningful to us. We planted pots for our windowsills and contributed energy, time and tools to the community gardens, areas of land that the council were happy to no longer mow, and that we were happy to use. Through doing this we were all able to use our alternative voices and enjoy listening to those of others.

Tim Maundrell, Shard End, Birmingham

The following page contaings Tim's refelctions in a diagram.

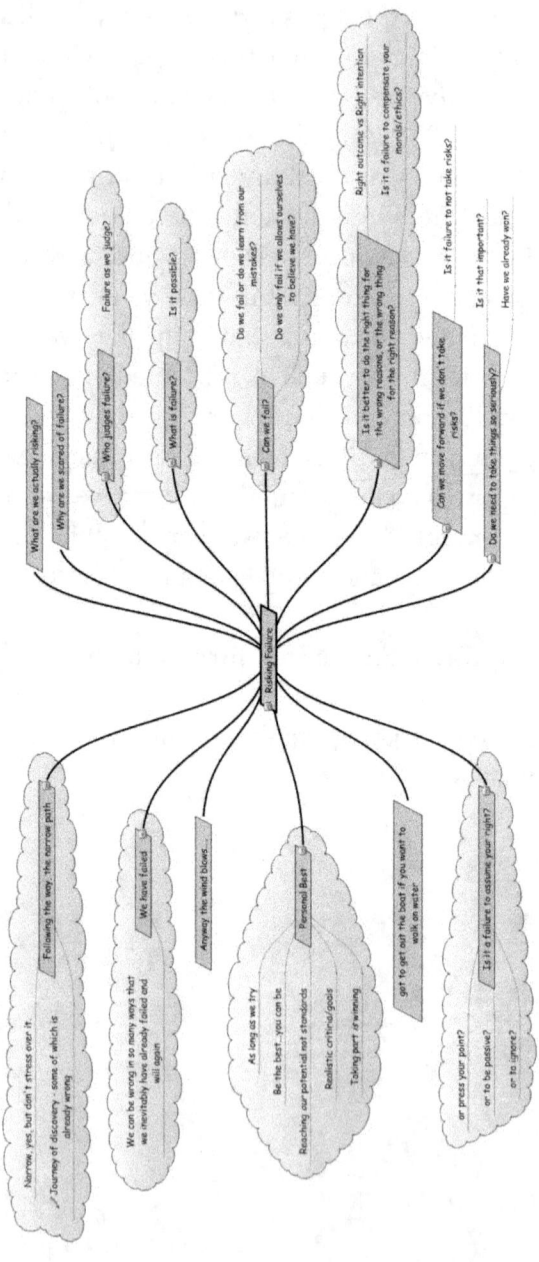

God our encourager,
you know the many things in which we're involved.
We offer to you
our frailty and fragility,
our fears and inadequacies
and pray that you'll use them all
to build up your church and world.

Sometimes we retreat onto safe ground,
keeping our borders well defended,
our protocols and policies in sharp relief.
And in doing that,
we forget the tender hearts
of the people around us
and their need of your presence in us.

Whatever we're facing today,
give us courage to be creative,
and take the risk of
opening our hearts and minds
to your pioneering Spirit,
recognising that you might call us
to do something new for you
and this neighbourhood.

Help us know that
no defence mechanism
however secure
can protect us from
danger and failure here.

But assure us in our deepest places
that we walk into today
with you before us, beside us and behind us.
And you, our God, are all we need.

Thank you God.

Lord, in your mercy
Let your kingdom come!

 We value courage, creativity and diversity as we try to discover relevant ways of being church in different contexts.

Freedom to fail offers permission to experiment and take risks, but courage is required to turn experimental ideas into reality. Courage is also required if the status quo is not to be automatically imitated. Mission strategies that work in suburban Britain do not always translate well into urban environments and yet refusal to adopt well-known methods often attracts confusion and criticism from onlookers, so strength of conviction and character are essential.

It might seem bizarre that followers of the Creator need to defend creativity with such vigour, but it does often feel quite rebellious to step outside the comfort zones the Christian community have made for themselves; to colour outside the lines of the dot-to-dot resources enthusiastically supplied by the respected Christian media-moguls. The latest programme or the most glossily-promoted project might offer helpful ideas but often these have been created in and for a middle-class, suburban context and therefore are likely to be less effective in other settings.

The task of those committed to incarnational urban mission is to either adapt these well-intended resources for their context or to create their own. The dilemma with both is that they take time and energy and those immersed in living amongst the disadvantaged often feel that they are at capacity and have few personal resources left to invest in such process.

Constant creativity is actually hard work and it is a discipline to choose creativity above predictability. Many regular preachers may find it hard to believe but during my time in Shadwell it was more time-consuming to devise a creative way of teaching and inspiring an unchurched, urban congregation than it has been in recent years to preach a monologue sermon to an established, passive, static congregation who don't answer back! In order to sustain creative thinking and action, a balanced life needs to be sought in which the mind has time to explore alternative ways of doing things and is fueled by encouragement from other creative thinkers. A lone creative is doomed to struggle if they are constantly the only one to offer alternatives, but place them alongside another creative thinker and they will thrive and contribute much. One of the joys of working in teams is this ability to bounce ideas around and dream together of alternate possibilities.

Because creativity is encouraged across the Urban Expression teams there has been a wealth of initiatives and ideas implemented. Because one inner-city estate can be so incredibly different from another this creativity means that the work of one team often looks very different to another. We have tried not to impose our own set of boundaries regarding what is expected but embrace the diversity which evolves as a result of this creative freedom.

At Street Level

Marg Hardcastle, Stoke

Just over a year ago a new extra-care apartment complex for people over fifty-five opened next door to our Baptist chapel. Called 'The Village' (although it's in the middle of the city) it's a modern building with one hundred lovely apartments, large reception lounge, community room and a café. Of course, it presented as a classic mission opportunity, but one that our small congregation could not take on alone, and one we didn't believe just 'belonged' to us either, so we sought to involve others.

We sent out a poster inviting people from the local Catholic, Anglican and Methodist churches to meet and discuss the possibility of doing something together. To my surprise fifteen positive and enthusiastic people came along to the meeting, representing all the churches and some residents. The proposition was put – to offer The Village a regular Christian gathering that wasn't labelled with any denomination, that was based around life-themes (rather than the lectionary), that involved coffee and conversation, that would be run by non-professional Christians and that would be inclusive and welcoming to church-goers and non-church-goers alike.

After the most positive grace-filled meeting I've ever been in, followed up with a meeting with 'The Village' management, 'Faith in the Village' was launched, twice a month on a Thursday morning. In the first twelve months it grew from a handful to forty regular attenders from within the apartments and from the local community. New people have been encouraged to lead sessions and others have had their faith re-enlivened. Some are experiencing 'being church' for the first time in decades. It is a simple format: we sing three hymns, listen to reflections on topics as diverse as sport, holidays and music, share prayers from the permanent prayer-tree in the reception area, and hear words from the Bible. It is a place to which we can invite people. It's friendly and relaxed and we share together in its running. Whilst it never set out to be, it looks like a church plant!

Although it's not the most 'out-there' mission ever done, it has involved a degree of courage, creativity and diversity. I didn't think anyone would come to the first meeting! If they did, I thought there'd be disagreement on the content and I wasn't sure The Village management would endorse it – but my fears were unfounded. No denomination has dominated but each brings a flavour of their tradition. Most of all, it is relevant to the context, the residents and the wider community – and it feels like 'being church' as opposed to 'doing church'. The content (particularly hymn-singing) isn't my personal preference, but it's what the local people want and enjoy. It's very different from any of the churches involved and it's enabled unity, grace and love to grow. And this summer a team from Faith in the Village took the initiative to organise a flower festival and café in the Baptist chapel, for two days, as part of the local community festival weekend.

So much, Lord, so much!
Talents, gifts, personalities, temperaments;
Histories, stories, influences, backgrounds;
All here in this neighbourhood,
this street,
this church.
So much to hold that it weighs us down;
So much to unlock that its potential is overwhelming;
So much to discover that it knows no boundary.

God,
help us to receive this diverse community
as your gift to us;
your creativity to celebrate
your people to love
your kingdom come.

And help us to see it as you do,
attentive to the parts that need mending
the signs of your coming
the glimpses of redemption

And help us to say 'Yes!' at the tops of our voices
to all that you ask us to be and to do.

Lord, in your mercy
Let your kingdom come!

 **We believe that questions and theological reflection are important as we learn together and so discern the way forward.**

In all honesty, the Christian community in Britain does not appear to be that comfortable with questions. We prefer to give answers, even to questions people aren't actually asking! Yet we live in a time when there are massive questions being asked about the very fabric of life alongside doubts as to the place and relevance of religion, and we need to create safe spaces to explore them, without fear of judgment and indignant indoctrination. Key attributes to assist this are an understanding of conflict and a commitment to dialogue and peacemaking. If we refuse to fall out because we think differently and if we enter conversations understanding that differences of opinion are acceptable, we are well on the way to creating safe space for questions and reflection.

One of the habits we have tried to incorporate across our teams is regular gatherings of team leaders so they can encourage one another but also refine each other's thinking and practice. These are intentionally not created to be opportunities to brag and boast (a characteristic of so many Christian leadership gatherings), but opportunities to be real, explore difficulties as well as share joys and ask questions of one another. I remember an occasion when one team that had been using shop-front premises for some years announced that they were going to start holding their worship gatherings there.

Originally they had explicitly declared they would only use the premises for more social and educational activities and felt that Christian worship in the building would be inappropriate. In the spirit of honesty and dialogue I remember quite a robust conversation taking place amongst the leaders as they helped the leader reflect on the reasons why their opinion had changed and explored with them the potential outcomes of this new direction.

One of the things Urban Expression has helped to develop over the last seven years is the Crucible course [30]. Originally in partnership with the Salvation Army NEO initiative and then their 614 movement,[31] this training programme was set up specifically to create space for those engaged in urban and creative mission to ask and explore honest questions about the nature of following Jesus on the margins of society in twenty-first century Britain. Exploring foundational topics such as discipleship, hope, evangelism and creating new churches – all from a perspective that assumes post-Christendom and urbanisation are integral contemporary starting points – the Crucible course encourages honest and real reflection. Participants often declare how free they feel to ask questions that they consider would be tricky to ask elsewhere

Urban Expression as an organisation is also learning and is trying to remain open to contemporary theological insights and practices which will cause us to

---

[30] www.cruciblecourse.org.uk
[31] www2.salvationarmy.org.uk/614uk

adapt the way we do things. In a context which is seeing unparalleled church decline, we know we cannot rely on traditional funding mechanisms in the same way many charities and Christian organisations do, and so we try to remain light-touch and flexible as we build appropriate scaffolding to support the teams. In a context which is exploring ethical questions too, we are also trying to remain open to what we might learn from one another – after all, at some point followers of Jesus have had to stand out and say that slavery and ethnic cleansing is wrong but that mixed-race marriages are not. With our limited understanding we have to remain open to what we might learn about our omniscient God and allow revealed truth to enable us to discern the way forward.

At Street Level

Stuart Murray Williams, Urban Expression coordinator and former church planter in Tower Hamlets

Many church planters and pioneers are activists and pragmatists, wary of being distracted by what they sometimes regard as unnecessary questions and impatient with theological reflection. They are more interested in what works, getting on with things and asking 'how' questions rather than 'why' questions. At least, that's how it seemed to be in 1997 when Urban Expression started. We launched this new mission agency because we were concerned that much contemporary church planting was replication rather than reproduction, uncreative and not contextual, programmatic rather than organic and presumptuous rather than incarnational.

We wanted to encourage pioneers to spend much more time listening to, engaging with and learning from the communities into which they moved. We urged them to be patient before initiating things and not to assume they knew at the outset what church would look like in their neighbourhoods. We expected them to ask lots of questions and to engage in ongoing theological reflection. One of the key roles of our coordinators and steering groups is to facilitate theological reflection.

I hope it is evident from the many contributions to this book that our teams have responded well to these encouragements. There are really significant theological reflections here, frequent testimonies to the learning that has taken place and many questions that team members are still wrestling with. Having a commitment to questioning, learning, discerning and theological reflection in our core values will, we hope, help us to resist the temptation to make unwarranted assumptions, be content with mere pragmatism or stop engaging with the challenges of an ever-changing urban context.

We are encouraged that church planting has evolved and matured over the past fifteen years. It is not just that many now prefer 'fresh expressions' or 'emerging church' to 'church planting', but that these terms indicate that more attention is being paid to context, culture and reflection on what it means to be church and to participate in the mission of God. Church planting accompanied by such theological reflection may be slower than the older pragmatic approach, but it is much more likely to result in contextually relevant churches.

Our God
you call us to a cycle of life
that involves growth, pruning, renewal and new growth.
As we engage our minds with your calling of us
we meet people and situations, issues and questions
that disturb us, provoke us, challenge us, deepen us.
Sometimes the questions can scare us
as they rattle our cages and raise anxieties.
Sometimes the questions can thrill us
as they make possible new things, new directions.
Lord in your mercy,
hold the questions we're living with today.
Infuse us with your peace
and help us to work with them
so that we become more truly yours, more truly ourselves
and more truly followers of Jesus.

Thank you for the people who help us to reflect well,
and those who give us the courage to deal with the consequences.
Thank you for our fragile communities
in whom you live
and grace with your hope.

Jesus invited us to a full and overflowing life.
Today we again gladly accept that invitation.
Grow us, prune us, whatever it takes
for your commonwealth of love to be known.

Lord, in your mercy
Let your kingdom come!

 **We aim to be catalysts, encouraging and releasing creativity in both church and community as we seek and share God in the inner city.**

Having freedom to be creative and think outside the box is not only beneficial for our teams but is something they can pass on, helping others to think of different possibilities, different futures. One regular characteristic of the communities the teams live in is that few residents believe that anything can ever change there. Feeling like they have little voice and no control over proceedings, people often descend into despondency and with disillusionment struggle to imagine a future for their neighbourhood, their family and themselves which looks any different. Facilitating opportunities for people to explore their own creative potential can enable them to see their wider potential to implement change.

The Geoff Ashcroft Community is an initiative set up by one team in response to the disproportionately high number of local people struggling with mental health issues. Those with the idea observed that those with severe mental ill-health often lacked opportunities to build meaningful relationships with others and suffered from low self-confidence. Through the humble beginnings of a weekly craft group the Geoff Ashcroft Community has enabled many people to build and maintain healthy friendships whilst also nurturing their creativity. One man in particular who began reluctantly to paint, has since developed a unique and personal style of art and had his work exhibited in several galleries in

East London. In identifying and releasing his creative nature he has also built his confidence and nurtured his soul.

Followers of Jesus are invited to have a glimpse of the future. As we explore and develop our understanding of shalom we see how things could be. Creativity lived out enables that future to become reality now, and the more others are invited to be part of that creative exploration the more they might see glimpses of their Creator too.

At Street Level

Jim Kilpin, formerly in Shadwell, London

Having lived in Shadwell for a few years we became very aware of the lack of play facilities for children in our local area. Shadwell is a densely populated community and very much a concrete jungle with limited space for children to play safely. There are far too many 'NO BALL GAMES' notices dotted around than is healthy for a community that in 1997 was able to claim over 75% of its population being aged under twenty-five.

We met a growing number of parents who would often comment how there was 'nowhere for their children to play' and 'nothing for them to do'. They also spoke warmly of a former adventure playground that was situated in the heart of the estate, which they used to play in when *they* were younger. That was some thirty-five years earlier, and due to changes in local government, and with severe funding cuts back in the 80's, the playground had closed with the gates remaining locked for almost two decades. In essence it was now nothing more than a wasteland surrounded by tower blocks, a dumping ground that had been left to rot, the former facilities having fallen into complete disrepair, with the undergrowth swallowing up what little former glory remained. It was nothing more than an eye-sore to any person who walked past.

In many ways it had become an indicative symbol of how people living in Shadwell felt about their community. 'Nothing here can change' was the popular response whenever we spoke with local people about 'doing something' in our neighbourhood, and as they pointed to the now unrecognisable 'playground' you could forgive them for thinking that too, as you stood looking at this haven for fly-tippers.

Then one evening, during one of our regular team prayer meetings, I had a growing sense that God wanted to challenge that misconception about change and was given a vision of the adventure playground being restored to its former glory. There was a very real sense of colour and life returning to the site and a sense that this in itself would become a symbol of hope to a community who believed that nothing could ever change. What would happen to the playground would be like a parable itself, showing how God wanted to bring new life and change into people's hearts. They too could know change in their own lives and circumstances.

Two years passed by and nothing happened, but the vision remained.

Then slowly, through a series of interconnected conversations, the opportunity to restore the playground presented itself. In collaboration with local parents and church members, and together with the Play Association of Tower Hamlets, an action group was formed to see the transformation of this dumping ground into a free, open-access adventure playground for local children.

After a further year of ticking boxes, raising funds, meeting requirements, and with much shedding of blood sweat and tears, Glamis Adventure Playground proudly opened its gates again to the local community after a twenty year closure.

It continues to meet local children's needs for play as well as providing a vital place to meet for many parents. It has become the heartbeat of the community, an oasis in the centre of an inner-city estate that once believed nothing could change. If you were to walk past today you could not help but be struck by the vibrant colour and the sense of life that transmits from this place, as children scream and laugh on rope swings, as parents talk over their cups of tea, or as stories are told around the campfire at night.

This, of course, is only half the story really. The ongoing conversations and relationships that were made by the church members through being involved in such a project saw people come to know Jesus. The playground continues to provide a precious place for those conversations to take place, even today, continuing to point many more people towards a God who believes that change really *can* happen.

(In 2007, Glamis Adventure Playground was awarded 'Best Adventure Playground in London').

Geoff Sims, East Bristol

'I wish I was creative.' An artist hears this a lot. Usually the meaning is 'I wish I could make things like that', interpreted as creativity. In truth, creativity runs far deeper than artistic competency. Declaring intention to 'release creativity' we mean far more than giving people paper and paintbrushes.

Creativity is part of humanity. The smallest children who discover the joys of a cardboard box, regardless of the expensive toy inside it, testify to the abilities of human imagination. We are made, declares Genesis, in the image of God. Not the tangible, physical image, for who can see God? The image of a creator God, with unique ability to imagine.

Creativity is key to our ability to have compassion, to understand each other. Millennia of literature, art and theatre attest to our capacity, even desire, to imagine the lives of others and thereby place ourselves within their stories. In a modern, media-driven age we are in danger of losing that ability. In a world where we have to be convinced by what we see on the screen or find it ridiculous, where self-image is shaped by advertising, where a click can give you all the information you ever want (and more) are we losing creativity?

Working in school I see the often staggering truth of

this loss; kids whose experience growing up in modern western society has squashed self-worth and hope. Children who revere nothing so much as celebrity, which society tells them is worthy of attention, but whose real achievement is to epitomise the image-conscious, fame-centred priorities of the age. What value would it be to these children to release their creativity? To allow them to imagine different goals? Possible futures?

As creativity is a divine gift we are given it to share for the benefit of others. Exodus 35:30-35 tells of Bezalel and Oholiab, 'filled with the Spirit... to make artistic designs for work in gold, silver and bronze' for the Ark of the Covenant, but not that alone. They were also given the ability to instruct, sharing their creativity that others might participate in Israel's worship, for creation of the tabernacle was surely worship.

What was the message of Jesus' life if not one of creativity? A reprimand to a society which, just as ours does, prescribed behaviour which made people feel worthwhile. In a world where obedience to the legalistic letter of the law (where leaving a beaten man to lie dying in a ditch rather than making yourself impure by touching him) was the only way to avoid condemnation from others, Jesus pointed the way to the true meaning of that law. A law demanding creativity and sensitivity to realise, not blind obedience. Jesus taught in parables, not dogma. Parables require imagination to interpret; without it we are merely hearing without understanding. So let's tell stories, listen to and encourage others to tell theirs, and let's encourage each other in the creative work of hearing and understanding the good news of the kingdom of God.

God we are alive and we thank you!
Your creative heart beats around us
In colour and sound, sight and scent.
We are blown away by your vision,
awed by your imagination
which is so much bigger than we could dream of.
But you have planted in us
an imagination that can soar to the highest places
and release in us gifts well hidden and under-used.
Our God,
let your Spirit unlock in us new ways
of thinking, of being,
of behaving, of creating,
and give us the eyes to see potential
in ourselves,
in others,
in our neighbourhood,
in our families.
And use us all to make the world
more beautiful,
more whole,
more integrated,
more centred,
more lovely
just as Jesus did.

Lord, in your mercy
Let your kingdom come!

 **We believe in discouraging dependency and developing indigenous leadership within maturing churches that will have the capacity to sustain and reproduce themselves.**

Some of our values have been easy to live out from the start, but this is one of those values we have included because we need to learn together how to put it into practice.

Whilst a foundational assumption of many mission agencies that focus overseas, the commitment to raising indigenous leadership is not so prevalent in Britain, especially in working-class, urban estates. This stems in part from our cultural assumptions that leadership is expressed most effectively by those who are middle-class and educated and that those whose life education has been received other than through higher education are destined to be recipients of leadership rather than instigators.

This is not an exclusive reality as some trades and professions show increased ability to raise such leaders, but there is evidence in our country of a shift towards elite leadership. 'There was once a tradition,' states author of *CHAVS*, Owen Jones, 'particularly on the Labour benches, of MPs who had started off working in factories and mines. Those days are long gone'[32]. He goes on to quantify this by saying 'Fewer than one in twenty

---

[32] Jones, O. *CHAVS, The Demonization of The Working Class* (Verso, 2011) p29

MPs started out as manual workers, a number that has halved since 1987' and then states the worrying truth that 'MPs aren't exactly representative of the sort of people who live on most of our streets'. This shift towards elite leadership is a danger that the church is not immune from and intentional moves to balance this might be helpful and strategic if the Christian community wants to remain connected with British society.

Raising indigenous leaders is not without its problems. An initial issue in some of our rapidly changing urban environments is the question of who exactly is indigenous? In parts of Tower Hamlets, for example, is it the third-generation Irish, the second-generation Bengali, the first-generation Lithuanian or the middle-class incomer who has lived there for twenty-five years? In other estates the answer might be more clear-cut as those who have lived there all their lives and those who haven't are easily identified.

The emphasis of this value is not so much the identification of who has been in an area the longest, but a commitment to looking beyond the usual presumptions about leadership and employing different criteria to discern who God might be raising up to inspire and lead others. Some of our teams have received criticism that the initial people benefitting from, being attracted to or becoming involved in whatever is developing are not the right kind of people on which healthy church foundations are built. One team that, even after a very short period, had built meaningful relationships with hundreds of people on their estate were advised by someone who was there to encourage them that they should be recruiting more middle-class, educated people from churches outside the area to come in and help lead things. Whilst resources from outside can be hugely beneficial and can help share the load, this attitude carried vast assumptions that there would not be leadership potential in this large group of local people.

A second issue is how to raise leadership without scaring people off! I remember a young lad beginning to follow Jesus in Shadwell. He was enthusiastic and passionate about his new faith and participated fully in all we did together. Trying to take steps towards releasing his potential we asked if he would take responsibility for ensuring there was someone to put the chairs out for one of our gatherings each week. Although he had been happily assisting with this task week in, week out, the responsibility felt too much and he backed off completely. He did not lack the competency but lacked the confidence to lead others and perhaps in our enthusiasm to be faithful to this value we had moved too quickly. Raising indigenous leaders is not simple and it is not always a quick fix strategy. Perhaps this is where choices sometimes have to be made between desire for and speed of church growth and desire to empower those who are often marginalised and overlooked.

Another team had a more positive experience and were able to disciple a young Asian student. After being part of this home-based, mission-minded, experimental congregation he announced his desire to become a minister and return home to Asia as a missionary. He has not, as yet, been able to return home, but continues to play a very active leadership role within the developing community of faith.

In another instance, a team leader decided to recruit his team as much as possible from the locality, rather than depending on those from outside. As a mission agency our recruitment process had presumed recruits would generally be moving in from elsewhere and that all prospective team members would be happy filling in application forms and coming to an interview. Our process, as it stood, was inadequate for this, but our underlying commitment to this value ensured we implemented alternative processes which enabled the same level of discernment and accountability that gave an alternative approach to identifying leadership.

At Street Level

Gary Serra Di Migni, Victoria Park, Manchester

Long, long ago, when working at the head office of a company based in the south, I visited one of our northern branches to advise them on their working practices. On the first evening I went for a meal with the staff. At one point everyone went to the bar leaving the manager and me finishing our meals at the table. The manager scowled. 'What's up?' I enquired. Pause... 'Coming up here, telling us how to do us jobs!' As you can tell, I've carried that evening with me for a long time!

Being an 'alien in a foreign land' wasn't an issue for

me when I was subsequently ordained, since my first pastorate was in London... and then came Urban Expression.

With Urban Expression's help, I discerned that God wanted me to start a church for people who wouldn't set foot in a church building; to enable local people to be church in a way that was relevant and authentic to *them*. It didn't matter where it was; it was a 'people group' I was called to reach – not a geographical area. Then personal circumstances and pragmatism pointed this Londoner to Manchester. Over and over in my head I heard, 'Coming up here, telling us how to live us lives!' I resolved to recruit my church planting team locally, rather than bring more southerners with me. However, this was about more than team. This was about succession planning, too.

What would happen to Urban Expression Victoria Park if God called me to do the same somewhere else, or on to something else entirely, or once God called me home? Would they or I bring someone else in from 'outside' – someone 'coming up here, telling us how to live us lives'? At least I'd had connections with Manchester since I was nineteen; through my wife, I had family here; I'd lived and worked in the area for eighteen months before I even started a Christian 'work' so that I could better integrate. What if, though, the next leader was born here, schooled here, fought here, grieved here, went clubbing here, and supported City (or even United)? What if the next leader didn't have to spend eighteen months *integrating*, because they already *were*? What if nobody would say to the next leader, 'Coming up here, telling us how to live us lives!', because s/he didn't come up here – s/he was already here; s/he'd drawn her/his first breath at Manchester Royal Infirmary? What if the church could see that you didn't have to talk like the Queen to lead a church? Wouldn't more of them step forward and say, 'I can do that?'

From my very first day in Manchester, as new people have come into contact with Urban Expression Victoria Park, I've asked God, 'Is this the One? And guess what – I think I've found One!

Loving Lord
you built your church with a mixed bag of people,
gentle, impulsive, schooled and uneducated,
men, women, young and old
and somehow through it all
you formed a community
charged with loving the enemy,
welcoming the stranger,
living with values
that others laugh at,
and all this so that the world might be redeemed.
We are part of that mixed bag
and while we struggle with its clashes
we rejoice in its diversity
and we're committed to it
because we've seen you at work
doing impossible things
in this crucible of love.
Help us to be attentive to those around us
who can be
holders of hope,
makers of peace,
catalysts for change
who can help shape our future life in good ways.
And help us, Lord,
to help them be all that you call them to be.

Lord, in your mercy
Let your kingdom come!

 **We are excited that God can be discovered in the heart of the city and commit ourselves to explore various forms of prayer and worship that are appropriate here.**

As well as being committed to not imposing forms of church that do not make sense in an urban setting, we want to discipline ourselves to find forms of prayer and worship that make sense too. It only takes a short time of living incarnationally and perceptively in an estate to realise how little sense many worship song lyrics make to many residents of an inner-city estate. Consider the following summary of the themes that recur in some of our most popular worship songs:

> The Lord's my shepherd and somewhere over the mountains and the hills you'll find me in the river that flows next to the trees that clap their hands, in which the birds sing sweetly, where all of creation sings to the fragrance of spring and the stars shine down and I feel like a flower in the mighty wind beneath the rainbow and in the silences I am aware that if I was a butterfly I'd thank you for giving me wings and I know you want to feel me and if I just wait upon you to touch me I am sure that there will be joy everlasting and you will be the air that I breathe forever and ever even though you are indescribable and incomprehensible.

Tongue in cheek, I know, but consider how much sense these concepts make to someone who perhaps lives in an estate where the multitude of high rises means there is no horizon, therefore no sunsets or rainbows, little vegetation and few butterflies, no silence… ever, little opportunity to hear the birds sing (except at night), too much light and traffic pollution to see stars, where cars, syringes and dead bodies are dumped in the rivers and canals, where some children have never crossed the city boundaries, where child protection issues are common and transactional relationships abound. Now read it again!

We are convinced that it is possible to connect with God in meaningful, worshipful ways that make sense in the inner city. The challenge is that it takes effort and imagination and some people who end up in our cities cannot be bothered to put the effort in and fall back on second-hand forms of worship that connect more with incomers who have experienced life beyond the city than those who have grown up here. We believe there is much to celebrate in our estates and our cities; God's presence is here in abundance. We just have to open our eyes and take time to look truthfully at our surroundings and our context.

The prayers at the end of each value are examples of an attempt to engage faithfully with street level spirituality and each team has developed their own local responses too.[33]

---

[33] One of our teams in Openshaw have worked over the years to produce street-level prayers and reflections which are available at www.dancingscarecrow.org.uk and in their book McBeath.C and Presswood.T, Crumbs of Hope (Methodist Publishing House, 2006)

Renowned urban missiologist Ray Bakke wrote *A Theology as Big as The City*[34]. This was a highly influential book for me in which Bakke challenges us that if our theology is not big enough to believe that God can make sense in the city and impact its inhabitants for good, then our theology is simply not big enough, full stop. If God cannot change the lives of people in our most deprived and challenging situations then I am not sure to what degree I can retain faith in such an entity. Likewise, if God is unable to relate to, make sense to and meaningfully connect with the urban contexts that half of his created human population find themselves in, I am not sure any worship song is worth singing any more.

At Street Level

Rae Pears, East Bristol

I've been looking at this value for about an hour now and I still am not sure what to say. I have been thinking why that is, and I think this because I am yet to discover the heart of God, and yet to see what prayer and worship look like here.

As the wife of a man who is training at the Baptist college here in Bristol and whose work and placement keep him in the heart of the city over four days a week, and then two days a week talking, reflecting and

---

[34] Bakke.R, *A Theology as Big as The City* (IVP, 1997)

learning about God and inner-city ministry, I have struggled to find my place. He has time to be there, whereas my time is filled with twins and a toddler, keeping the house as clean as I possibly can, cooking food and making sure I don't go totally insane, and I feel there is little of me left to really even think about God, or what we are doing here in Easton. What time I have left has been taken up with some difficult church situations in the last year too, and my desire to engage spiritually with anything has been non-existent.

A few weeks ago there came a point when I knew I needed to see some change. Our community meal was happening while Andy sat outside with a guy he spends a lot of time with – he has been in care all his life, struggles with drugs and alcohol and gets himself into a lot of trouble. As the evening progressed I got more and more frustrated. It turned out this guy was refusing to leave, threatening to smash a brick through our window and lying down across our path. I began to realise I felt nothing but anger towards this man, and worse, I was embarrassed that my neighbours would see this and worried what they would think about it. I worried that he would come back whilst I was here on my own with our three girls and demanded that he never came back to our house.

I know that it's OK for me to feel scared about this guy coming round again, which since then he has, and he has been fine. But what shocked me was how little regard I had for him – and he isn't just one guy – where we live there are literally hundreds and people just like him. How can we as a family continue doing what we are doing if I respond like this every time? How can I expect to find God here if I see only the issues this guy has and not the hope God has for him?

Since then, I know I need to open up my heart and allow God to show me his heart and hope for this place, but I know it's going to take some time for me to see it. What has been inspiring me, though, is meeting others with the same passion as us for this area, people who genuinely love living here and love God. Through those conversations I begin to hear God's heartbeat here, and I begin to find my place in all of this. For me that starts at toddler groups, engaging with other mums, listening to the good and the bad in their lives and opening up our home and ourselves to build honest, good relationships. My hope is that this will lead me to engage more with our community, and start exploring what prayer and worship look like here in the inner city of Bristol.

Steve Tinning, formerly of Harold Hill, London

In the churches I've been part of, I have often been involved in the 'worship group'. My guess is that most Christians would understand that to mean I play an instrument, or that I sing, or in some more progressive churches, that I might have the necessary IT skills to work a projector or sound desk. All of these, admittedly to varying levels of ability, are basically true. Yet my understanding of worship has never been comfortable within these constraints. I have always tried to think imaginatively about worship, shaping it to the context of those taking part. Moving to Harold Hill and being part of the Urban Expression team there, left me facing new questions in this regard.

Is sung worship practically appropriate here? Very few would know even the most famous church songs, many would be embarrassed by singing in such a small and personal group and the phraseology in the songs would be completely inaccessible to them, considering their limited literacy levels and almost non-existent understanding of theological concepts. How could we adapt worship to make it more familiar and accessible to people in this urban context?

One example of how we have tried to address this happened last Christmas. Just about everyone was looking forward to Christmas and we wanted to embrace that sense of anticipation. We thought lighting the candles of an advent wreath each week at the community meal, and focussing our prayer and worship around the elements of the wreath, would be a good way to do this. But what might an advent wreath look like in the urban context? Surely a motorbike tyre would be a more familiar sight than evergreen leaves! So we took a small tyre, cut holes in which to place four candles and sprayed it metallic green.

Of course, the evergreen leaves of a conventional wreath would represent life even in the depths of winter – hope in the midst of difficulty. Our wreath was to reflect this too. It was covered in items and pictures that members of the community had brought. These things represented that which gave them hope and life, and each week we thanked God for his provision for these things.

A simple act, a communal act, and although there was not a word sung, people were brought before God in gratitude, without feeling alienated by an inaccessible mode of worship.

God of the city,
You are here in
the lives of the people,
the bricks of the buildings,
the pavements we walk on,
the scrub ground we pass by,
the trees in the park,
the voices in the market,
the hopes and dreams
of all our neighbours.
We thank you for that.

Give us the eyes to see you at work
and minds that can quickly glimpse
your growing kingdom.
And when we see it,
help us to sing an Alleluia!
A jazzed up, street sourced Alleluia!
A grating, soaring, garage Alleluia!
A rap, urban, Bangra Alleluia!

You are the beginning and end of our worship
and we want to worship you honestly and boldly.
Help us to work out ways of worship and prayer
that aren't borrowed ways
but ways that our community,
our environment,
our churches
are aching to express.

Give us eyes to see and ears to hear.
Alleluia!

Lord, in your mercy,
Let your kingdom come!

 **We realise that God's Spirit blows freely and so we will not assume our work should continue indefinitely.**

When Urban Expression began in 1997 we were not sure it would last one year let alone fifteen! We were acutely aware of the risks we were taking and knew that success was not guaranteed and so were prepared that in the case of failure the work would need to cease. Almost one hundred volunteers later and in a phase of positive recruitment, it does not appear that Urban Expression will need to stop anytime soon because of lack of interest. Indeed, with sister organisations emerging in other countries it seems more likely that we will need to establish new ways of relating and learning from one another in the coming months.

However, this does not mean this value has become redundant. We feel it is important to regularly ask the question as to whether Urban Expression should continue or not. In a post-Victorian/Christian society many of us frequently have to make painful decisions about bringing the work of a society, congregation, brigade or club to an end. Some of these institutions have surfed the crest of their wave and have been cruising down into the foam for decades, yet the assumption that their work should continue forever has paralysed them from asking whether it is time to cease or not.

It is a bizarre idea that every organisation should last forever and that its closure signifies failure. None of the churches the apostle Paul planted exist today, yet we don't talk of his failed mission!

Urban Expression as an organisation or movement will not last forever and we want to remain open to discerning the right time to conclude or morph into something new. If the question is on the agenda this prevents it from becoming the 'elephant in the room', the question that cannot be asked or the deathly words of a doomsday prophet. It offers, instead, the opportunity to review things and look ahead proactively and positively, embracing daring creativity as we look ahead. In fact, we ask this question quite regularly and ponder whether it would be more effective for Urban Expression to continue a little while longer as it supports the establishing of new teams or whether it would be more effective to cease and see what adventurous alternatives start as a result.

We also encourage our teams to ask this question at a local level. Some urban communities change so rapidly that it is only fair to ask if the work of a team or congregation is complete or if it needs to continue and, if so, in what shape. In fact, when a team has completed the task of morphing into some expression of church we encourage them to graduate from Urban Expression anyway and join another relational network of churches if they haven't already. We do not want to become a denomination as there are already plenty to choose from! We would rather retain our focus as a mission agency that serves the existing denominations and networks.

At a local level these questions probably do not contain much reference to Urban Expression as an organisation, as local teams may well adopt a more relevant local identity or name. Whilst as an organisation the question is always whether we are still effectively recruiting, equipping, deploying and networking teams, at a local level the question will hopefully be whether God's kingdom is still being sought and experienced, whether people are discovering a new relationship with Jesus and being inspired to participate in God's mission. If and when it becomes apparent that in ceasing we would encourage more of this, we will embrace the challenge and plan a great send off!

At Street Level

Phil Alexander, Shadwell, London

We live in a fluid world. A world in which people are constantly moving house, switching career, beginning and ending relationships or just changing their minds. Instead of planning for the rest of our lives, we are told to ask no more than, 'Where do I want to be in five years?'

When my family and I moved to Inner London, the number one question we were asked was, 'How long do you plan to live there?' My wife was told by a well-meaning minister that the inner-city church she had just become a pastor of would be a good 'first church', presumably in her ministerial career!

The problem with this approach is it makes urban ministry ineffective and unfulfilling. As Urban Expression

Mission Partners, my wife and I believe we are called to genuinely be part of pre-existing communities. We did not move to the inner city to create community, nor did we come to work with the community. We came as outsiders and asked to be welcomed and included. Such a request cannot come with a time limit. Many inner-city communities are already familiar with those who come for fixed periods of time. They recognise that to live in the inner city is, generally speaking, not anyone's first choice and fully expect those who come from outside to move on reasonably quickly.

So then, if a fundamental tenet of the Christian call is to live counter-culturally, we may feel our duty is to go against the trend of continuous change and make outrageous promises to ourselves, and others. We may naturally pledge the rest of our lives to the urban setting to which God has brought us as it feels like that is what He would have us do.

However, to do this would be to close our minds to the voice of God as He constantly shapes and directs us. God's Spirit does indeed flow freely as God cannot be bound by His own creation nor is His creation completed. We believe God called us to the community in which we live but we also believe He calls us daily to make countless choices and enter into new situations and that one day that call may be like that given to Abraham – to gather up our households and move to a completely new and unknown place, not to start again, but to continue an ongoing adventure in partnership with a loving Father who knows our potential and how best to bring it out of us.

Imagine God's creation as one huge jigsaw puzzle and each of us as pieces in that puzzle. The pieces always fit together but God is constantly reshaping individual pieces in such a method that the way in which they fit is never quite the same. Eventually a piece that started in one part of the puzzle may fit better somewhere else entirely than in its original place. The jigsaw can no longer be put together in the way it once was without disrupting a large number of other pieces and hence distorting the picture the puzzle displays. As the pieces within the puzzle change and move, so the picture changes and becomes more perfect.

And so my wife and I live and work with open hearts and open minds. We are aware that God's hand is at work in our community and at present we are instruments of that work whether this continues for our whole lives or for a fraction of that time. God will always be found in our community even if one day we are not. We pray that we will always be found working with Him wherever we best fit into the puzzle.

Jayne Irlam, Victoria Park, Manchester

Fin was led into the medical room by two police officers and flopped dejectedly into the chair in front of me. I was the forensic nurse charged with the task of assessing if he was fit to detain. He had already made one attempt on his life, and now sported the police-issue 'suicide vest'. He hung his head with the air of someone who literally couldn't take any more of this life, whose self-esteem had been bludgeoned out. I could see deep scars down puny arms, injection sites and cuts to the wrists, fresh and lurid.

As I began to talk to Fin, I had that strange experience I was beginning to recognise. I looked at this young man, made in the image of God, so full of latent promise and so badly scarred in body, mind and spirit, and my heart went out to him. Or perhaps it was not really my heart, but Christ's. I began to gently clean up his wounds and talk to him. My standard nurse's agenda dissolved into something deeper, much more powerful; I felt the Spirit move in me, take the words and make them His own. I also experienced my own internal struggle; I didn't really want to witness Christ in front of the officers, but the impetus grew larger than my selfishness. I began to talk of Him to Fin. Some time before, Urban Expression Victoria Park had set up an informal referral service from police custody into the local Christian rehabilitation centre, and as I told him about it, for the first time he made eye contact with me. Just for a moment, a flicker of hope lit them and he agreed to accept a referral.

After Fin had been led out, I did my usual thing of praying that the Lord would protect me from any backlash for being so 'politically incorrect' as to witness in the workplace. One of the officers entered the room and, very solemnly, asked if he could speak privately to me. Oh no, I thought, here it comes. He closed the door, sat down and tears slowly filled his eyes. He had listened to my speech aimed at Fin and realised that he too had need of this Saviour; could I introduce him? In that moment I realised that the broken exist everywhere, in all sections of society. And while we are busy deciding who needs Him, the Spirit works where He chooses. These two men, separated in society by a huge socio-economic gulf, were nevertheless united by their need of Christ. And in their finding of him, could become brothers as they entered the kingdom together.

Living God
thank you that you don't leave us simply maintaining
ways of worshipping,
ways of meeting,
ways of being your people,
but that your invitation is to an abundant,
overflowing life.

Help us to see our lives in seasons
when there is a time
to sow and reap,
to plant and establish,
to harvest and enjoy,
to prune and wait.

What we do is all yours.
You are our guide, our leader,
our protector, our nourisher.
You build up and you tear down.

Help us not be so attached to what we do
that we miss your voice saying
'Enough!' or 'Move on',
But in all that we do,
and in your mercy Lord,
help us to hear your voice saying
'Well done, my good and faithful servant,'
because when times are hard
we need to know that this matters to you.

And it's only because all these people
and all their situations matter to you
that we are here at all.

Bless us Lord, we pray.

Lord, in your mercy
Let your kingdom come!

CORE VALUES – RELATIONSHIP

 **We believe that, in Jesus, God is revealed locally, and that we should be committed to our local community or relational network and active members of it.**

Without the logic of 'Missio Dei' (as explained in the Core Commitments) it is easy for some who follow Jesus to be deceived into thinking that only a few specialists are invited to join in with God's task of revealing Divine love to people. People can mistakenly conclude that only those who are ordained, or in leadership, or who are in some kind of paid position of employment with a congregation or organisation are responsible for sharing in this mission. They are the ones expected to give up their free time and be available at all hours to 'follow their calling'. Everyone else might feel it is perfectly reasonable to focus their free time and energy solely on their immediate family and friends, prioritising their own emotional, relational and social needs.

There is nothing wrong in focusing attention on our families and friends. Indeed, many people flee church life because it consumes so much of their precious time and prevents them from actually maintaining healthy relationships with their loved ones. However, the invitation to be a light to the nations, to go to the ends of the earth, was an invitation for all who have been changed by God. All of us live our lives in a context, networked with people through the rhythms of work and life. This might be a context which we have strategically chosen, but more often than not it is a context we have stumbled into. Whether we have chosen or stumbled into this context we have an ongoing choice about the level to which we engage with it. Even those who have intentionally moved into urban neighbourhoods with Urban Expression have a daily choice of whether to open their eyes to see what God is doing there and how actively to participate in it.

This value simply encourages all of us to be observant to what God is doing and what the God who sends is asking us to join in with. There is no person, no community, no network, no day, no time in which the Holy Spirit is not actively looking to reveal the love of God to all humanity. If we are actively committed to those we are with we may well spot what God is doing and be able to join in.

At Street Level

Graham Kerr, Possilpark, Glasgow

How I see God revealed locally is hugely dependent on my commitment to, and involvement with, my local community. However, I did not always understand what commitment was. In the past I felt a certain contentment that because I lived in the community my church was located in, that I was committed to my community. I had mistaken proximity with commitment. Being committed to our local community, as I have discovered, is much more than being within a certain distance of where the church meets.

I think it is vital that we have the mindset of being on mission even if we are in our own country, and maybe especially if we are. If we believe we are on God's mission wherever we are, then we should be prayerfully preparing ourselves to understand the people, the place and God's purpose in that community. Whilst this may involve study of languages or customs for missionaries going overseas, in urban communities there are local customs and languages which we need to become familiar with too. Therefore we require the same preparation and training when working in any community, even if it is only a couple of miles down the road.

If we understand the people, we can see where God's love is revealed in their attitudes and actions, as well as identifying areas where His love needs to break through. How a place is regarded by the people living in the community is often different from how it is regarded from the outside. Living outside the community doesn't give as clear an understanding as living inside the community. Praying knowledgeably about the situations and circumstances specific to our communities, 'in situ', helps us to see God's purpose in our context more clearly.

It is very easy to live a life isolated from the community we are called to serve in, even if we live in the area. If we commute in and out for work, family and social activities it can be very easy to live in a bubble where we are numb to what's happening in the community.

I believe it is not enough to just locate ourselves in a community. To be effective and bear fruit, living in the community must be joined with the determination to make the community our home: to find out how the heart of the community beats and beat alongside it; to find the rhythms of the community and follow them too; to have the courage to cling to what we must not let go of, or we would cease to be who God wants us to be. To have the humility to let go of the things that create a barrier between us and the community; to partner in the sufferings of the community, speaking out against the oppression and injustice, and praying down the manifestations of evil seeking to steal and destroy. To partner in the joys of the community, speaking out to encourage and strengthen the love and truth, and thanking God for the manifestations of His kingdom which are present bringing life and hope. I seek ways to be involved in the community so I can see my community as my home, my neighbourhood and my mission field.

It is important to feel committed to our communities with our hearts as well as our heads. When I hear my community being criticised or derided by people outside the community I feel a sense of injustice. I believe that I shouldn't be unaffected by this. Rather that it would be insincere to distance myself from my community by thinking 'I'm only here because I'm on mission.' We must share the sufferings and joys of our community and this is what will happen naturally if we are truly engaging with it.

I believe God is at work in my community. But I will discover more clearly how He is working here if I am an active part of what is happening. There are ways that God is blessing the community that I will only see if I am willing to be blessed by them. There are struggles that the community is facing that often don't get shown to those outside the community and only if I am willing to identify myself as a member of the community will I be trusted with them.

Whilst I was thinking about this I had a picture which I thought summarised this. There was a real plant and a plastic, artificial plant, both sitting in the soil side by side in a garden. Both looked the same when viewed from outside the garden, but to those who were in the garden the difference was obvious. The real plant had vibrant colour in its flowers and provided a beautiful fragrance into the air. It was growing roots into the soil and breaking through the clay it was in. It offered pollen to bees and nutrients to insects; it was also transforming carbon dioxide in the atmosphere into oxygen. The plastic plant didn't have any fragrance or pollen, or nutrients. Its roots could not break through the soil and it couldn't bring transformation or produce any oxygen. Most importantly the real plant was growing and the plastic one could not. I believe this illustrates the difference between a church being committed and active in the local community and a church that is not.

Marie Larvin, Stepney, London

Being committed to my local community means realising that the most important thing is not where I can buy stuff cheapest, or where I can get the best quality, but recognising that I have the choice to support the local economy where possible, by doing my bit to keep someone in business. It means knowing that when I walk the two minutes to the shops by us I will bump into people who I may only say hello to… today… but that after saying hello a few times, and then talking about the football, and then what's happening on the estate… we may then have a shared connection point to bring the kingdom of God to Stepney. It also means I can go in my slippers and no one's going to bat an eyelid!

It means getting my haircut in the local hairdressers and seeing God at work in the lifeline that this regular contact gives to a lot of our older and more isolated residents – but it also means knowing I am likely to hear talk of the 'Pakis' and be faced with the dilemma of how best to respond, how to show something of the Jesus who worked to break down those barriers and prejudices that have existed down the ages and continue to inflict painful wounds.

Being committed to our local community means I'm embarrassed that I don't know who lives at numbers 7 or 20, and feel inadequate that it seems too late now to knock on their door and ask. But being determined to get to know the new families moving into numbers 15 and 17 – which means we now have someone in our block who can water our plants when we're away – fantastic!

Being actively involved in our community means that the Community Fun Days and Christmas Events are now partnerships between the local Residents Board, the Housing Association and E1 Community Church. Not always an easy partnership, but better to be involved than not.

It means making the choice to have a girls' night playing bingo at the estate social club or watch the football at the local pub and see God at work in the conversations that spark off… including the addition to our little community project *Helping Hands* of a man who, after one too many one night at bingo, volunteered to come and join in with what we were doing, and is now a regular!

Being committed to our relational network means that the annual Easter Egg Hunt is now attended by over eighty people. People look forward to it, in the weeks leading up to it they talk about tactics for winning it, and are now willing to sit and hear about God's love for them. It means there are loads of children and young people from all different backgrounds that know there will be something going on for them through the church community during school holidays…

And occasionally people 'come to church' too!

God,
we come before you just as we are
with all our frailties and vulnerabilities,
our baggage and prejudices,
our hopes and dreams,
our life and love
and we offer it all to you.

Take all we are and hope to be.
Use us here where you've brought us
and help us to be like Jesus.
Use our hands, our eyes, our ears,
our words, our silences,
our work, our rest,
our hearts and minds,
and let your kingdom come
in the lives of all who live
next door and round about,
in this street and square,
in the whole neighbourhood.

Confirm in us your invitation
to be your people here.
Deepen our commitment to it.
In our experience of the
heights and depths of life here
help us to know your surging and renewing love.

Lord, in your mercy
Let your kingdom come!

 **We believe that the gospel works through relationships and that serving God consists largely in building life-giving relationships with others.**

The Gospels tell us that Jesus came to bring life in all its fullness[35] and he did that by moving in and living amongst the people he created and loved. In its simplest form this is what Urban Expression teams seek to do too.

Some might suggest that Jesus would have been far more effective had he chosen to live on earth in the twenty-first century when social media would have facilitated the communication of his message and life in an instant. The news of the death of Whitney Houston on 11 February 2012 is reported to have been tweeted forty-two minutes prior to being announced by the first traditional news outlet and provoked one thousand tweets per second[36]. Just imagine the effect this technology would have had on the story of the life, death and resurrection of Jesus!

As it was, Jesus came and lived amongst a particular group of people at a particular time and immersed himself in a limited context, building relationships with those he met. In an age where scope, success and reach are so eagerly measured and quantified, it seems to go against the grain to choose to enjoy the small, the

---

35 John 10v10
36 Flemming.H,
http://www.blackenterprise.com/news/whitney-houstons-death-impact-on-twitter/ posted February 15 2012 Accessed 16.07.12

seemingly insignificant, the unnoticed. Yet it is in immersing ourselves in a context that we can develop eyes to see what God is already doing and join in. Quite often Urban Expression teams begin with a specific identifiable 'patch' in mind, but it is interesting how many end up narrowing that geographical area down to an even smaller neighbourhood which they feel called to immerse themselves in. As the sphere of influence decreases, perhaps the scope of potential increases.

One of the challenges facing missionaries who go abroad is the ease with which they can remain connected with home. Although a deep blessing in so many ways, it can also be a hindrance when 'missionaries don't leave home behind anymore'[37] but continue to receive their emotional support from the other side of the globe via the internet. So often this can feed the unhealthy Christian missionary psyche that it is their job alone to give to those they are 'serving'. They can feel that it is their responsibility alone to give to 'the other'; to support, to encourage, to nurture. Yet it is in developing a two-way, life-giving relationship that glimpses of God are most frequently and beautifully seen. If a missionary receives all their 'life' from friends thousands of miles away, they might not have their eyes open to discover it in those on their doorstep. Likewise, those serving in our inner-city communities need to resist this psyche and allow themselves to be open to receiving the life that surges towards them from those they share their lives with.

---

37 Duckworth, J. and Duckworth, J. *Against the Tide, Towards the Kingdom* (Cascade Books, 2011)

Of course, we hope that churches will be centres of life-giving relationships, and many are. However the fastest growing section of the Christian community in the UK quite probably consists of those who have left church, or are in the process of leaving. It is worth honestly acknowledging that, whilst many of those who have adopted a 'churchless' faith cite reasons such as losing their faith or falling out with people, others say it is because they wanted to avoid burnout, were discouraged and felt few resources were offered for life outside of the church subculture.

These claims need to be taken seriously and we need to ensure that any new forms of Christian community we create genuinely explore what life-giving relationships truly look like rather than fall into default soul-sapping modes of church.

At Street Level

Lizzie Gilmour, Possilpark, Glasgow

I left my mum with my baby on the pavement and went to unlock the flat. As I reached the door I realised I had locked my keys inside. Not the greatest of life's trials but I was tired and emotional from the new world of motherhood and I went straight into meltdown. As I stood close to tears and using some remarkably colourful language, a friend in the community who had been exploring faith came round the corner. My heart sank even lower. I didn't want her to see this side of me!

This experience highlights a half-hidden belief I carried into Urban Expression with me. It's the belief that we need to become infallible or at least hide our weaknesses from those who do not yet know Christ. When we build 'life-giving relationships' we are the ones offering life. Aren't we?

As I have lived in the inner city these last few years this belief has been challenged. I have frequently found the roles reversed. I am the one who doesn't have it all together. I am the one on the receiving end in the 'life-giving relationships.'

Is it OK to need help from others? Jesus seemed to think so. He was supported by a mix of people. He received financial support from wealthy men and women. He was reliant on others for a place to stay. He spent time unwinding with friends. He was ministered to by a woman who anointed him with perfume shortly before his death. And in the hour of his greatest need in the Garden of Gethsemane he asked his friends to stay near him. They were witness to his tears and turmoil.

Can unbelievers be those people of strength for us? Jesus was not so quick to categorise who was a believer and who was not. He frequently challenged people's assumptions telling those who thought they were 'in' that they were 'out' and vice versa. In one shocking example he told a Roman Centurion that he hadn't seen greater faith than his in all of Israel. A Roman Centurion! A man in a leadership position over the movement that was oppressing the people of God. Jesus saw God at work in people from all walks of life and built relationships with a wide range of individuals.

What if Christ is at work in the lives of both believers and unbelievers as he seeks to draw them closer to Him? What if it is in fact He who is the Life-Giver and not me? This is a great leveller. Suddenly I am not so different from my neighbour who does not yet know Christ. We are both helpless. Equally in need of Christ's transforming love day to day.

Perhaps it's appropriate to mention how I eventually did get back into my flat. My mum went to get a taxi to pick up spare keys from the letting agency. When she arrived she happened to meet the manager of both companies. On hearing what had happened he insisted she sat down. He then sent one of his drivers to pick up the keys while she drank a coffee. When the driver returned he would only accept a reduced fare. This man is renowned for his involvement in criminal activity yet I can't help but feel we received something of Christ from him that day.

As I work out this value in my own life I am learning to be slower in my judgments, more honest about my limitations and more open to receiving, as well as sharing, the Gospel message.

Alison Shorter, Harold Hill, London

Relationships are about people, about time, energy, commitment; about sharing in each other's lives. A relationship is a two-way thing and it doesn't work if it is only one-sided.

I guess when I joined Urban Expression I would have read this value in a slightly different way. Then my focus would probably still have been about the life I, with God, could bring to the relationships I was part of. Now I definitely see how God brings life into relationships from both sides, those who know him and those who haven't quite seen him yet. God can use all of us to bring life – at the end of the day He's God and He's in control of how He shines His life and light into lives. Maybe some of us are aware at times of how God can use us in this process, but I think most of the time God watches and sees how life is being shared and smiles. I am sure He smiles first when He sees the sharing of life, second, when we notice, and a third time when we miss it completely but He's on the move!

I believe that God has shown me, through the way Jesus lived, that relationships are about giving life and I want to try and live this out where I am. Moving to a new place, getting to know those around me and sharing my life with people has given me the chance to share the Gospel. As we live alongside one another we encourage the good in each other's lives, support where we face challenges and most of the time just walk along together knowing that we are not alone. As I've leant on friends around me God has used them and shown His love through them, but He has also allowed me to be used in similar ways. One example of this is our recent kids' club. The families we know asked us to run a kids' club which we did for children aged five-eleven. However it would have been really tricky with our two year old about. I chatted about this with some of the mums and a couple of friends offered to look after her while we had their older two children at the kids' club. It was about community working together.

This Urban Expression value is about bringing and receiving life. In our community, I hope that I have made, and will continue to make myself vulnerable to God and those around me so that God can continue to show His gospel through the lives of people.

God,
thank you for all those that you've placed in our paths,
for the sorted and the centered,
for the muddled and bemused,
for the broken and the fractured,
for the searching and confused.
In all our relationships
let the piercing light of your love
infuse us and flow through us,
challenging the depths of the darkness,
offering the hope of new beginnings,
providing warmth where hearts are cold,
giving strength where wills are weak.

In us and through us
let all those we meet today
be touched by your Spirit,
and may we see your presence
reflected in the faces of
friends and strangers.

Lord, in your mercy
Let your kingdom come!

 **We recognise that Christian faith is a journey and we are committed to helping people move forward, wherever they are at present.**

One of the characteristics of contemporary church life and mission in Britain that has come under question in recent years is the relationship between belonging, believing and behaving. There have been multitudes of discussions and papers on this topic especially in academic circles, that may have been helpful in developing our thinking.

It has certainly pushed our notion of what some call 'bounded' and 'fuzzy' sets of belonging, but it is not always clear what this has meant in practice in many of our Christian communities. Anyone with any significant experience of urban mission under their belt knows that people's lives are messy and complicated. As Britain becomes less 'Christianised', the vast majority of people's lives also look increasingly less like the perceived Christians of yesteryear, so messiness and unpredictability is perhaps becoming more predictable. In this context it is vital to have realistic expectations of what discipleship might look like and what the variety of starting points might be.

Those working amongst people of other faiths are often quickest to embrace the concept that enquirers may need to belong deeply to a Christian community before they can explore belief with integrity, and that some behavioural aspects may remain unchanged until faith deepens. However, those working in more monochrome contexts sometimes find this harder to embrace.

There is something here about the question previously raised of whether we love someone because we want them to become a Christian or whether we want someone to become a Christian because we love them. If we lean towards the former, we may quickly lose patience at someone's inability to change the way we think they should or the speed with which they change. If the latter, we may feel able to remain committed to helping someone even if their lifestyle choices make us feel uncomfortable or challenge our preconceived ideas.

The value of recognising faith as a journey is that it also helps to remove the whole 'them and us' issue. Whilst I have made reference to enquirers exploring their faith and journeying towards lifestyle changes that we hope might reflect their new found faith in Jesus, the truth is that we are all on a journey of faith and none of us has yet achieved perfection! An attitude which implies that 'they' need to change but I do not is not only unhelpful but also denies our own discipleship needs. I need others to help me learn about myself and the more meaningful relationships I forge the more I am exposed to my own frailties and failings, my own prejudices and fears. It is then that I become aware of my need to move on in my faith journey and practice and do so as an equal partner with everyone else.

I remember one occasion when a man who had been recovering from many years of drug and alcohol addiction confessed to me that he had slipped and spent the weekend drinking with friends. He knew this was not something that was wise for a new follower of Jesus and he was deeply ashamed and repentant and asked for forgiveness. I assured him that he was forgiven, that he would learn from his errors, that Jesus didn't judge him and neither did we. I could have left it there and felt like I had done a good job at discipling him, however that weekend I had been out for a night with a bunch of girls and had drunk a couple of glasses of wine too many. I knew I had overstepped my usual limit and whilst I had not done anything too embarrassing, I felt that as a follower of Jesus and as a leader I had not set a good example. I did not need to confess this to him and knew there was a risk that he would look at me differently if I did, but his honesty and integrity inspired me to confess my errors too. At that moment we became aware that we were fellow travelers, sharing the same forgiveness and hope, able to encourage one another along the same path and, as long as we were moving forward more often than we were moving backwards, we were doing OK.

At Street Level

Juliet Kilpin, formerly of Shadwell, London

In an attempt to build deeper friendships and expose local people to life outside of Shadwell, I helped organise a church holiday to a large house in the countryside. After a well-attended weekend thoughts turned to organising a similar event the following year, however we knew the country house would be too small if numbers continued to grow.

One of our neighbours suggested that we organise a trip to Butlins. Butlins is a holiday camp – a quaint British institution with a reputation for cheap accommodation, all-round family entertainment plus a bit of extravagant indulgence of the alcoholic and amusement arcade variety! Having previously only been to Butlins when it was colonised by the Spring Harvest Christian festival, where all traces of secular tackiness were replaced with Jesus-junk, I was a little uncertain about the idea. However, I concluded that this was a local idea and an environment that many local people felt comfortable in, so agreed to organise the first of what would become an annual trip to Butlins.

One of the things that hindered people going on holiday in our estate was the lack of banking resources. It is very difficult to pay for a holiday when you have no bank account and no credit card, so a receipt book and money bag became my constant companion as I collected regular contributions towards booking fees.

Each year, after numerous last minute changes and crises, a whole load of us boarded a coach and set off for Bognor. One year there were ninety of us! So began fun-filled weekends of variety shows, cabarets, amusements, sports tournaments, games of crazy golf and karaoke. Each year we arranged with Butlins to use one of their vacant rooms so we could meet together as 'church' and do something vaguely spiritual. As a congregation that never met on Sunday mornings, it was the one time in the year we felt that 11am on the Sunday was actually the optimum time to gather – late enough for people to have woken after a night of heavy drinking, but early enough that they might not have started again!

On these occasions we were acutely aware that most people were not regular church attenders so we made every effort to contextualise the experience as much as possible. We shared breakfast, told stories about Jesus, heard testimonies and even sang a couple of songs (we were getting into the flow of karaoke of course!). We then facilitated a practical response and on this occasion it involved deciding if we wanted Jesus to be our rock and writing the day's date on a stone as a symbol of our decision.

We departed for home with hangovers, cuddly toys, empty purses and stones in tow!

Several people took great pride in showing me that they still had their pebbles when I visited them in their homes. It obviously meant something profound to some. Later that year one of the older ladies who had been to Butlins sadly died. Having conducted the funeral service I was sitting quietly in the front seat of the hearse en route to the cemetery. From the midst of the grieving relatives behind me a shout came from the lady's daughter: 'Oi, Juliet! You know we put mummy's stone in wiv 'er! It meant a lot to 'er. She'd've wanted it in there!' Christian faith is definitely a journey and I was pleased that this lady had come to know Jesus as her rock. What the crematorium staff thought of its presence in the coffin, however, I'm not sure!

Our God
we are a part of that great crowd of people
who are learning what it means to abide in your love.
We thank you that we are not alone in our journey,
but from the beginning of human experience,
right through Scripture,
right through the stories of faithful people
you have invited us to travel with you
in this journey of salvation.

We recognise the journey takes us
through desert landscapes
sometimes dotted with oases,
sometimes arid, dry and forbidding
as far as the eye can see;
through beautiful landscapes
filled with water, trees, sky and hills
where all creation cries Alleluia!;
through urban landscapes,
noisy with change yet a place
where nothing really changes.

We offer you our journey and pray
that, while you lead us to where we
need to go,
you'll help us to be fully present today
to your Spirit,
ever beckoning,
ever calling
ever inviting
to life in all its fullness.

And we offer to you the faith journey
of those we know,
praying for them your peace and hope,
and an ever deepening awareness
of your love and life.

Lord, in your mercy
Let your kingdom come!

 **We focus on under-churched areas and neglected people, trying to find ways of communicating Jesus appropriately to those most frequently marginalised, condemned and abused by society.**

It is a worryingly remarkable achievement when a nation gets to the point where the majority of the population feel marginalised. The unemployed youth, those with disabilities, those from Black and Ethnic minorities, the elderly, those with mental health illness, faith groups, secularists, the lesbian, gay, bisexual and transgender community, married couples… all have been reported in national news sources in recent months to feel marginalised.

So what do those of us in Urban Expression mean when we talk about those most frequently marginalised, condemned and abused by society? I guess this value leaves us open to focusing on a wide range of people, for who cannot say that they sometimes feel neglected?

Our attention to under-churched areas is an acknowledgment that whilst technically every parish has a 'church', there are geographical areas that have multitudes more than others. This might be as a result of bad planning or population change, or it might be that some places have been prioritised by evangelism and mission strategies more than others. Whatever the reasons, there are swathes of urban Britain that have very little church presence for the number of people that live there. When we moved to Shadwell our research showed two small Anglican congregations, another almost closed Anglican congregation, a large Catholic congregation and two independent congregations. Perhaps this sounds sufficient until you note that the population of Shadwell was 30,000 at the time.

In Britain we live in a society where 6% of people regularly 'go to church'. In a belated but positive move recent figures have started to look at data for attendance at mid-week expressions of church also[38]. These slight additions are encouraging, but barely dent the statistic. The implication is that there are numerous people groups that remain unchurched, unconnected in any meaningful way with a Christian community. Urban Expression is keen to identify such groups and intentionally work beyond the fringe of inherited church to connect with those who might be intrigued by the Jesus story.

Within this parameter we also seek to prioritise those most frequently overlooked. One example of this was when one team began to notice how they were attracting and connecting with a large number of people with mental health difficulties. They were a small and fragile team, stretched in many directions as they sought to build community for their diverse neighbourhood. At one stage it felt as though the friends with the most obvious mental health difficulties were a distraction, preventing them from focussing on building a church community as originally intended. How were they ever going to plant a recognisable church if they had to spend

---

38 Goodhew, D. (Ed) *Church Growth In Britain: 1980 To the Present* (Ashgate, 2012)

all their time caring for these needy individuals?

When the issue inevitably reached a crunch-point the team sought counsel, and as they embarked on a process of prayer, dialogue and discernment, came to a point of peace, accepting that God wanted them to prioritise those who might often find church a place of misunderstanding and rejection rather than welcome. Whilst some onlookers remained confused about their counter-cultural choice, the team remained convinced and the clear focus enabled them to build a beautiful, if alternative, expression of church.

All of the teams have sought to discern who the overlooked and neglected are in their neighbourhood or network, and have made choices to lean towards inclusion rather than exclusion. Whether that has meant embracing the sex worker, the foster child, the addict, the manic depressive, the self-harmer, the cross-dresser, the immigrant, the head-lice infested, the incontinent or the confused, each team has tried to remain faithful to the one who prioritised those on the margins.

At Street Level

Rob Schellert, Hackney, London

Some time ago I ran into a friend who lives on the street, in front of where I live. He was standing there looking at a motorcycle that was parked in front of the building. I walked by and he asked if the bike belonged to me. I said 'No, I wish it did though!' The next thing I knew, he started to tell me everything he knew about the bike that was parked in front of us. He went on to describe each part of the bike down to the tiniest detail. We continued to talk for some time about our day-to-day lives. It turned out that he had been taking acting classes at the local community drop-in centre. Apparently they were working on a play in which my street friend played the part of a pregnant woman. I would love to see that, I thought to myself! He must have read my mind as he invited me to come along and see him and his friends perform the following week.

The next week I went down to the local drop-in centre expecting to see my friend perform in a play that he and his friends were working on. When I showed up I quickly realised that there was going to be no performance, but an acting class instead. Since my friend had not shown up yet I thought it best to stick around just in case he appeared. Eventually he showed up and before I realised what was happening, I found myself participating in the acting class alongside everyone else there. My friend was so thrilled that I showed up that he introduced me to all his friends at the start of class.

As the class began, the teacher reminded everyone that the main objective of the class was to be on time. Apparently, timing was everything. If we were not in the right place at the right time everything could go horribly wrong! Now, I thought to myself, this isn't a real acting class if the main objective is to be on time. The teacher announced that we were going to practise doing some improv that day. She asked for three people to share something that they had seen or experienced that week.

A few raised their hands and shared what they experienced, then we were split into three groups and told to act out how we thought the three stories played out based on what we heard.

I couldn't really tell you what the stories were about but they pretty much all involved girls, drugs, booze, guns, fights breaking out and someone getting hit by a bus. This is surreal, I whispered to myself. The teacher would come by and watch our improvs and make suggestions such as making our actions bigger and more dramatic. So I found myself making my actions of smoking a spliff larger than life and going over the top in the scene that involved getting hit by a bus. Towards the end of class we all had to share our improvs with the rest of the groups and talk about what was good and what could have been better.

The teacher asked if I would be coming back. I wondered if she assumed I was poor or even homeless. But at any rate, I realised that I am actually on the poor side according to society's standards, so I could keep on taking these classes if I wanted to. After all, I felt right at home with my new found friends.

This comical incident got me thinking about creative ways we can engage with the poor and homeless on their level instead of having an 'us and them' mentality. More than anything I want to be their friend rather than some guy playing the part of a hero trying to save them from the streets.

So much for the idea of being an outsider coming in to see a performance!

God
we pray for all Christians in this place that,
as yeast in the dough,
you will use us to be a transforming presence.

We confess our own labelling of those
who are not like us;
our standing apart from strangers
as we surround ourselves with friends.
We are sorry for the ways in which we
scaffold up the walls that divide us
and pray that you'll give us a
vision
of this community
fully reconciled,
redeemed
with the
rubble of walls
building places of
meeting and eating
together.

We pray for all those who are
most neglected and
most unloved;
those used as

scapegoats
for the
deeper sin
which besets us all.
Help us to challenge
wrong attitudes
and
destructive behaviours
and in our churches to create
communities which are
truly inclusive,
filled with
justice and peace
and flowing with
life-giving love.

And God,
where the old ways of introducing
people to Jesus seem to have
lost their power,
ignite our
imaginations
and give us
courage
to share his life in ways that
truly connect,
truly empower,
truly transform.
We ask for this, because we have
no-one else to turn to.

You are our God
and we are your people.

Lord, in your mercy
Let your kingdom come!

 We challenge the trend of some Christians moving out of the cities and encourage Christians to relocate to the inner cities.

There is an urban tsunami taking place right now. The warning sirens are sounding and are being heard loud and clear by many world leaders and global enterprises. It is now an undisputed fact that there are more people in this world living in cities than not and there are a substantial number of cities today that simply didn't exist ten years ago[39]. What was once considered an optional interest for poverty-concerned charitable types is now a non-negotiable for all because urbanisation now impacts everyone, whether they live in a city or not. The urban lens has to be the dominant window through which we look if we want to understand how the world functions and respond appropriately.

But is this siren being heard by the church? One would hope that the church might be concerned about the well-being of the population of the world in a practical sense and might be on its marks to help prevent the dystopian levels of poverty predicted, but even if it is not so concerned about such physical matters, one would think that a global church that is seeking to 'reach the ends of the earth' with its message of spiritual renewal would see the sense in prioritising cities. After all… most people live here!

39 BBC News Interactive Map: Urban Growth
http://news.bbc.co.uk/1/shared/spl/hi/world/06/urbanisation/html/urbanisation.stm Accessed 16.07.12

Therefore it would seem to make sense that any strategy for humanitarian aid, whether that is physical, emotional or spiritual aid, that does not incorporate a strategy for engaging with residents of our cities is doomed to failure. So Urban Expression is seeking in some small way to echo that siren and inspire people to respond.

Of course there are many inner-city residents who are desperate to move out. In fact, there might be considerable expectation for them to do so. One resident of a Manchester estate observed to a team member 'If you move here you are seen as a hero, if I stay here I am seen as a failure.' The urban challenge extends not only to those who might move in, but to those who might want to resist the urge to move out. Interestingly, most waves of immigration begin in our inner cities and then move out over the ensuing decades. Many urban congregations in Britain are benefitting from the presence of Jesus followers from Africa and Eastern Europe, and this is a significant factor in the cautiously celebrated statistics about church growth, but it will be interesting to see whether this flow remains in the inner city or trickles elsewhere.

Of course whilst over one hundred people have moved into some of Britain's inner-city communities with Urban Expression over the last fifteen years, not all can stay forever. Some have moved to other equally challenging situations (East London made a good training ground for Beirut, Lima and Pakistan it seems!) and some have decided that urban mission is not a long-term choice for them. Some have needed to take a break but hope to return again in the future, others have found their urban experience painful and need time to reflect and recover.

We do not want to make people feel guilty for not moving into the inner city, or for moving out. We do, however want urbanisation to shape significant decisions that are being made at macro and micro levels by all faith-based or secular organisations. If urbanisation is not shaping strategic decisions for the world then our strategies, however glossy and sexy, will be inadequate for the world on our doorstep.

Reflecting on his experiences at the United Nations Conference on Sustainable Development Rio+20 in June 2012, CEO of the World Wildlife Fund, David Nussbaum says:

> 'The science is clear. We have to revolutionise our current development model, where we're living beyond the capacity of our planet, and don't equitably distribute the rewards and resources. And we have to do so quickly if we're to avoid the more serious and expensive potential consequences of delay.'[40]

The fact that most of the world's population live in cities and will continue to do so for the foreseeable future, has to impact our creation and implementation of

---

40   http://blogs.wwf.org.uk/blog/business-government/business/rio-reflections-the-politically-possible-versus-the-scientifically-necessary/ Accessed 16.07.12

sustainable development. Fortunately, there are many people who intuitively understand our urban communities at a grass-roots level. If they were invited to work alongside those who understand global urbanisation, perhaps many mistakes could be avoided and new solutions inspired.

At Street Level

Shona Kerr, Possilpark, Glasgow

When I became a Christian I started going to a nearby church. I found it difficult to integrate with my peers because I was one of the few people who actually lived in the local council estate and didn't have Christian parents. At first I felt shame that I had a different background and upbringing. It took me time to realise that it was not God's intention that I should be ashamed of my culture or disown it. It also took me a while to make the connection that many of the parents of my peers were brought up in council estates. When they had become Christians they had saved hard and moved themselves and their children out of council estates with intentions of protecting their children from the difficulties they had experienced growing up and giving them better than what they had. This motivation is honourable, but due to the cultural differences and the difficulties I had integrating, I found it hard to bring my family, friends and neighbours to church. I realised that if a church is seeking to journey with a particular community, or subculture within that community, it must actively bridge the cultural gaps. The reluctance to bridge the gaps often stems from a fear that core Christian distinctions will be forsaken, but I believe it is possible to bridge the gaps without forsaking these. If the gaps are not bridged, the community is vulnerable to concluding that they do not belong or are not welcome in the kingdom of God.

How can a church bridge the cultural gaps to the community? It is possible to bridge some of the cultural gaps by serving the local community faithfully over a long period of time. There have been many Christians who have selflessly and faithfully served communities and have addressed many gaps, but it has taken decades. I have become more convinced through my experience of living in Possilpark that it is vital to live in the community you are reaching. I believe this gives us the greatest potential to bridge the cultural gaps. There is no better way to learn about a community and understand it than living there. Living in a community because we are on mission, however, is only the start of the journey. Over time the community must become our community or the community will sense we don't feel at home with them. I believe, as we follow Christ's example by being incarnational, it gives us greater authenticity to speak to the community about Jesus. I also believe it gives us greater authenticity to speak on behalf of the community to the church, helping shape the church into its cultural context.

I have often heard people who are serving God in the UK toil over where to live on the premise of investment, reputation or local amenities and the view from the windows. Whilst these are genuinely valid considerations I am concerned that they are more influential than they ought to be. I reckon that this is one of the main reasons we have seen a haemorrhaging of Christians out from the cities. Many local communities and church congregations in the cities are under-represented and under-resourced. I think this situation has been further perpetuated as the communities have experienced a decline in Christian presence. It seems the more deprivation has grown, the more the Christian presence has declined.

I believe the only way we can address this is for us to invite God into the decision-making process of where we live. I do not think seeking God about where to live is only for those of us who are called to serve God overseas. Something seems to have gone wonky in how we disciple people if only those leaving the UK are encouraged to seek God's guidance about where to live and own the word 'missionary'. We must stop assuming by default that where God calls us to serve is not necessarily where God calls us to live. Our access to personal transport has enabled us to separate 'the living' and 'the serving' very easily. I believe this has warped our understanding of incarnational ministry in a way that has allowed us to claim this title, without giving the same level of commitment and sacrifice that many generations of Christians before us did. I believe that if more of us invited God into the decision-making process then there would be a redistribution of Christians throughout the UK, and as a result we would have a stronger presence in the inner cities. Until that day let us be encouraged that those of us in the inner cities are like Gideon's army; little in number, but the Lord is with us in His mighty power.

Alex Ellish Alexander, Shadwell, London

I love the inner city like a changeable lover: one day enthralled, besotted and adoring; the next day moody and unresponsive. I'm heady with the sound of Bangla music floating on the air; my stomach rumbles with the wafts of cooking curry coming through the window; my eyes gorge on the colours of the city, the shower of fairy lights from a high-up window, long dresses and salwar kameeze sweeping grey concrete pavements. Days when I feel like I know what I am doing here, days when I feel like I am being 'useful', days when I feel increasingly entwined in people's lives in positive and community-creating ways.

Days when, as I walk around, I realise I'm in love and everything is as it should be.

Then there's the other side, when I only see the flaws in my beloved: the hum of The Highway that keeps me awake and restless on warm summer evenings; rubbish and litter punctuate my walk home; days when sirens, screams and never-ending noise is the soundtrack. Days when I really don't know what I'm doing here; days when it's clear that no matter what I do, I can't change some situations; days when I want some room, some space, some privacy. Days like that when I want to run and hide, go somewhere clean, safe, gentle.

But I can't leave this place that I love and struggle with. I have seen too many moments of beauty and shocking love to walk away. Sometimes I fantasize about other 'safe' places that I have lived in, but I visit them again and I shudder. I can't go back there. I would miss the vitality, the rawness and the mystery of life in the city.

I often feel truly sorry for Christians who can't imagine living in the city – they are missing out! Missing out on moments of connection and grace with people so different from me. Moments when time slows down: when beauty, tenderness, pain and connectedness whirl and melt into each other so you can't tell one thing from the other.

I had a moment like this a few months ago as I embraced a beautiful woman that I might not see again. As I put my arms around her to thank her I was surprised to feel her embrace me back. And as I said 'thank you' and whispered 'God bless you' into her neck and hair more than her ear, I felt that spark of mutuality, of being more than just two people who got to know each other at a mums' and toddlers' group. We hugged, kneeling on the floor together. She was fighting back sobs and not looking at me to try to hide away her tears, but in that moment we knew something deeper about how we as people know and are known. We understood something in our faiths in Allah and God, and the working out of those faiths that bound us together as sisters. We were mourning the end of a season in both of our lives. Mourning friendship and companionship that will not continue to blossom. Mourning missing out on watching our children grow. Mourning the loss of laughter and kiwi fruit on a Thursday morning.

That embrace was one of the reasons I came to the city. To meet and be bound up with people I might not have met otherwise. And for those moments, both sweet and painful, I whisper thanks to God from the depths of myself.

God our hope,
you have called your people
to live lives of fullness
throughout the world.

We pray today for brothers and sisters
who find it hard to live that calling
in the inner cities and who,
wearied or frightened,
crowded out or isolated,
have clashing aspirations
and seek what they don't have somewhere else.

We pray for those facing questions today
of whether to stay or go
and ask that you guide them in their discerning,
fill them with your love
and give them a vision
for your city redeemed.

Let your people come here and grow here
and may we be the community they need
for them to flourish and fulfill the potential
that you have given each of them.

Let your church grow!
Let your people be free!
Let your kingdom come!

Lord, in your mercy
Let your kingdom come!

 **We believe in doing things with and not just for communities, sharing our lives with others and learning from others who share their lives with us.**

Many inner-city communities in Britain are fed up of having things done to them – the latest government campaign, the next bright idea, the new regeneration scheme, the new wave of do-gooders. Over the decades long-term residents have seen these initiatives come and go – usually on a three-year basis when the funding runs out or the next government gets elected – and it breeds frustration and cynicism. Being aware of this, we wanted to do what we could to ensure that Urban Expression would prioritise working with people rather than importing and imposing our own ideas, and seeking to honour the cry of the urban poor: 'Nothing about us, without us, is for us'.

This has meant taking the art of listening seriously. Many of us are activists and would feel justified imploring others to not just sit there but do something! However, in taking this value on board we try to give ourselves permission to not just do something, but sit there! Often teams will commit their first year to intentional listening, taking time to be present, to observe and to get to know those whose experience and wisdom can help shape what is to come.

This is such a valuable process and many teams have found it imperative that as wide a variety of people as possible are heard, not just other Jesus followers. It is also vital that listening is done with a genuine desire to hear and allow the truth of what we are hearing to impact what we eventually do together. It is no good 'listening' having already decided when, how and where you intend to 'do church' or feeling pressurised to comply with what sponsoring agencies require of you.

During our first year of listening in Shadwell it became apparent very quickly that on Sunday mornings our estate was like a ghost town, apart from the few people popping out to the local shop in their pyjamas. It was not difficult to conclude that gathering on a Sunday morning for church would be inappropriate if we genuinely wanted to connect with those in the neighbourhood. Of course if we wanted to attract Jesus followers from elsewhere it might have made sense to start something in a way that regular British Christians could understand, but this was not our goal so we had to think beyond the usual parameters.

At Street Level

Hannah Batchelor, formerly in Stepney, London and now in Troydale, Manchester

Meet Cal, mid-thirties, with a child the same age as my youngest. We first met at a local baby group and discovered that we lived on the same estate – the estate where my husband and I had moved to minister incarnationally. Cal is a bubbly, out-going, hospitable person who loves to serve.

As time went on and our friendship developed she

would often tell people about the work I had been doing in the community, with young people and the Tenants and Residents Association (TRA). She would say that others should get involved more and take an active role in tackling the problems they liked to complain about. I encouraged her to come along to the TRA meetings, which she was reluctant to do due to restrictions placed on her by her partner.

Over time her partner has come to trust us. We were the first people that they allowed to look after their daughter. Since then we have regularly looked after each other's children, fed each other, offered practical support and advice to one another. She recently baby-sat whilst my husband and I went out for the evening and remarked on how thankful she was for the peace and quiet. This situation brings to mind the story of Elijah who received hospitality and sustenance from the widow at Zarephath; in turn she received life beyond all expectation![41] In putting ourselves in her debt our friend has received life. Where is the power in this relationship? What are we offering beyond our need of help with looking after our children? I have found that I now have the permission to speak truth to this woman. We see this played out when Jesus takes the time to seek help from the woman at the well.[42]

Finally I was able to persuade Cal to come along to a TRA AGM after she had volunteered at an estate fun day and helped with an activity for young people. She made

---

41 1 Kings 17:7-24
42 John 4:1-26

some great suggestions for community events and activities. We encouraged her to run with one of those ideas. She took the lead in ideas and preparation for the event and, I believe, found release in being able to do things that she loved and would love to do as a job one day. The event was a great success and we plan to do it again. Here was an opportunity to empower her to take a lead in pursuing the things that she cares about and to draw in the involvement of the section of the community that she represents. I feel that she is now an ally that I look to for ideas and support in the work that I do in the community.

God our shaper
thank you for calling us into community
in this community.
Thank you for its colour and vibrancy,
its texture and life.
Thank you that we can't do all that you've asked of us
on our own.
But it's together with all the people here
that we're asked to build your commonwealth
of justice, peace and fullness of life.

We offer to you our hopes for this community
and name them before you now.

(pause)

We pray for partners in this community
with whom those hopes could be made real
and name them before you now

(pause)

We pray that you will take from us any pride,
any assumption that we know best
and that you will give hearts open to
receive your word and life
from the friend and stranger we will meet today.

In all our work, keep us humble,
conscious that without you we are nothing
and without our neighbours we are a clique.

Bless our partnerships and our dreams and let your kingdom come!

Lord, in your mercy,
Let your kingdom come!

 We see teamwork, networking and mutual accountability as vital, recognising that individuals and churches need each other.

Human beings are intrinsically relational beings. We need each other. Other people make us richer and help us learn about ourselves and most often those least like us help us to learn the most. Someone suggested to me that is why God made Adam and Eve so different from one another!

In one of our Crucible week-ends we explore the topic 'Becoming Human'. We investigate issues of discipleship and ask how we can respond to the way society constantly disciples us and how this contrasts with the way of Jesus. In our increasingly individualistic society we ask what role we have in discipling one another through authentic two-way relationships and how we can walk towards becoming the people we were created to be.

To be fully human is to be who God made us to be, but in order to become fully human we need each other. This concept is summarised beautifully in the African word 'Ubuntu'. In a lecture given by the Forgiveness Project[43] on 12 May 2010, Archbishop Desmund Tutu explained the concept. 'Ubuntu', he says, 'is the essence of being human. Ubuntu says I am because you are. I

---

43 www.theforgivenessproject.com Desmond Tutu's comments can be viewed here http://www.youtube.com/watch?v=cb2QyvYN24w Accessed 16.07.12

can't be me unless you are you. I need you in order for me to be me, as you need me in order for you to be you… Our humanity is bound up in one another's.'

It seems obvious to us therefore, that teamwork, networking and mutual accountability are completely vital to our journey of understanding more fully the nature of God and becoming fully the people we were made to be.

Tutu concludes: 'Hatred and revenge are corrosive of Ubuntu. Forgiveness and reconciliation are the essence of Ubuntu.' Team work and relationships of all kinds are not devoid of conflict. In fact if you want to avoid conflict it is best to remain on your own! As we commit ourselves to team and to working relationally we also commit ourselves to being prepared for the inevitable conflict, being prepared to deal with it creatively and honestly with dialogue, proactive listening and truth, ready to forgive and be reconciled with those with whom we disagree.

At Street Level

Iona Jones, Cobridge, Stoke

Last week at ROC Café Cobridge[44] we unveiled a 4ft square mosaic which had been created by forty-one young people and volunteers. It took about six months to complete and looks amazing.

The mosaic was the brainchild of our friend Frank

---

44 www.roc.uk.com

McGregor who is a community artist and a Church Army officer working from the local Anglican church. We work with him at his Messy Church[45] project and he volunteers for us at the ROC Café which meets weekly at Cobridge Community Centre.

Frank offered to create a piece of art with the young people based on the ROC Café Cobridge logo. He spent a long time planning the mosaic, meticulously marking each square on a board. He collected hundreds of different mosaic tiles, smooth or ridged, plain or sparkling, plus lots of mirror tiles to reflect the light. Some colours fitted the logo design but there were many random others for the young people to choose to make their own design for their particular square. Nothing was rushed in the planning.

Some were very keen to contribute to the mosaic while others had to be gently persuaded – they weren't sure if it was a cool thing to do. Some chose to make their mark with particular colours – Port Vale or Stoke City. Others styled their initials or just liked the way particular tiles looked next to each other. Some worked on their own and some in groups. This wasn't a quick win project. It took six months from start to finish. It needed patience, determination and considerable faith.

Frank is so creative and skilled that he could have made the mosaic easily, and much more quickly, by himself, and the physical results would have been similar. He could have been proud that the design was exactly as he had imagined. There wouldn't have been

---

45 www.messychurch.org.uk

any clashing colours or slightly out of place tiles. It would have looked perfect.

But what a waste of an opportunity it would have been. Young people and volunteers worked together, watched the mosaic taking shape and felt proud of their creativity, which some thought they didn't have. The personal impact on the contributors during the process and particularly at the unveiling was priceless. If Frank, or any of us, had done it alone, as beautiful as it could have been, it would have been just one person's work.

The mosaic is fixed to the wall in the main hall at Cobridge Community Centre. The names of those who made it are on a key at the side of the mosaic. People looking at it recognise the names of their neighbours and friends and see how creative and collaborative they've been. The process and the end result clearly show that 'Two [or many] people are better off than one, for they can help each other succeed' (Ecclesiastes 4:9).

Alex Milne, Leyton, London

My wife Astrid and I work together to lead a small community called 'The Vine' that meets in our front room in Leyton, East London. Due to the lack of a larger team we feel limited in our ability to expand the ministry. We would like to see other groups established in other homes. Recently a relatively new believer who has only been to some of our meetings has shown a willingness to occasionally host The Vine in his home. I want to disciple this individual. Maybe he could become a future leader within The Vine.

We would love for the community itself to be more of a team, but many in the community are struggling with their own personal issues. We want to see our members set free so that they are able to serve more. I have been developing links with The Healing Rooms, an initiative just round the corner from where we live. The Healing Rooms are prepared to train people up to serve on their teams and I plan to join their team possibly with some Vine members and then feed back the things we learn to the rest of The Vine.

Through speaking with other Christians I have been able to learn about different ministries that have been able to help The Vine members. I was able to take one of our members to Choices, a Christian crisis pregnancy centre. I have also taken another of our members to a Christian organisation called Remar where he entered a Christian drug rehabilitation programme.

Astrid and I belong to a group called a 'huddle' which is an accountability group within the Order of Mission.[46] We have found this extremely helpful. The huddle, made up of eight to twelve mature Christians, has provided a place where we can share our struggles and have members of the huddle pray for us and listen to God for us. I have found this helpful in keeping a balance in my Christian life. For years I had developed a lifestyle that included too much fasting, but to begin with I did not see it as excessive. I just thought I was being obedient to what I thought was God's promptings. It was prophetic revelation through some of the huddle

---

46 http://www.missionorder.org/

members that convinced me that I was fasting too much. This area of my life is now more in balance.

On Sunday mornings my family attends a New Wine church that is four miles away from where we live. This has been helpful for our own spiritual lives. We have taken some of the members of The Vine to their events and I believe they have benefited from this contact. I used to take some of our members to the Anglican church in the evening but this was sometimes difficult because our members could be noisy and disruptive. One of the members of the Anglican church said of The Vine, "We need you." I think she meant the church needed the challenge we all brought to a relatively comfortable, middle-class church. The Vine now meets on a Sunday afternoon or evening and is developing its own identity.

Thank you God
for bringing us together,
working as a team,
held by a vision,
committed to a way
of living and working
in which Jesus is known.

We readily confess our need
of support and encouragement,
of honest listening and talking,
of friendship and laughter,
of each other.

Bless each of our relationships,
and help them to reflect
the depth of relating
known in the Holy Trinity –
    mutual, flowing, life-giving, abundant, free.

God, we're human enough to know
that sometimes relationships become strained.
Wherever this is true for us,
may your reconciling Spirit
work among us,
repairing and deepening
our mutual understanding
respect and love.

God thank you for this team!

Lord, in your mercy
Let your kingdom come!

What now?
Stuart Murray Williams

You have reflected on the twenty-one core values and seven commitments that are at the heart of Urban Expression. Well done! You have journeyed with many of our team members and mission partners as they have shared their stories, passions, weaknesses, experiences, joys, sorrows and ongoing questions. You may have joined in the prayers that we pray to ensure that these values and commitments are matters of the heart, not just a collection of worthy statements.

What now? You may already be involved in urban ministry, in incarnational mission, in pioneering activities. We hope this book will encourage you and offer you resources you can translate into your own context. You may be considering getting involved in the kinds of communities and ministries you've read about here. We hope this book will help you discern the call of God and identify some of the issues you need to explore. You may know some of the people who have contributed to this book. We hope you will have a better understanding of what they are doing, and why, and will be more able to support and encourage them.

What now for Urban Expression? We are still a young and fragile mission agency. As many of the contributions to this book acknowledge, we still have a long way to go before all the aspirations in our values and commitments become realities. And we need to keep these values under review – the version used here is a revision of earlier versions and we will no doubt want to revise it again in the future as we continue learning about urban mission. There may be shortcomings and weaknesses in these values that we have not yet recognised – feel free to point these out to us if you can. And there may be values or commitments missing that we need to add as we continue to reflect on what we are learning.

We hope it is evident from the many contributions in this book that our team members and mission partners have been shaped, inspired, challenged and nourished by our core values. They are living and lived priorities, albeit imperfectly lived out. But maybe we need to go further and deeper. A few years ago we wondered whether we should identify Urban Expression as an 'urban mission order'. We knew a number of other communities and mission agencies that had adopted this way of thinking and operating, and we were aware of the growing popularity of 'new monasticism'. We talked and prayed about this for several months, concluding in the end that we should not move in this direction, but recognising that many of the 'marks of a new monasticism'[47] were already evident in our lifestyle, practices and relationship.

47 The twelve marks of new monasticism can be found at www.newmonasticism.org

But recently we have been challenged to move beyond 'missional values' to 'missional practices', and this may be something we need to give attention to in the coming months. What practices do we need to develop and build into our lives and into Urban Expression as a missional community that will enable us to live out our values more consistently and radically? It may be that some of these practices are already operative in different teams, so that we can learn from one another; or we may need to experiment with fresh missional practices that will enable us to live out our values and commitments more creatively and faithfully.

May we invite you as you reach the last page of this book to pray for Urban Expression – that we will remain true to our values and commitments and open to whatever God calls us into as we journey on – and to pray that you, the reader, will discern your part in the great mission of God?

APPENDIX A: BIBLICAL REFERENCES

Some years ago Karen Stallard produced a version of the core commitments with Biblical references. These are not 'proof texts' to justify our convictions but resources for further reflection.

Mission Statement

Urban Expression is an urban mission agency that recruits, equips, deploys and networks self-financing teams pioneering creative and relevant expressions of the Christian church in under-churched areas of the inner city.
(Acts 1:8)

Commitments

We are committed to following God on the margins and in the gaps, expecting to discover God at work among powerless people and in places of weakness.
(James 2:1-9)

We are committed to being Jesus-centred in our view of

the Bible, our understanding of mission and all aspects of discipleship.
(John 13:15; Ephesians 4:15-16)

We are committed to seeking God's kingdom in the inner city, both by planting churches and by working in partnership with others in mission.
(Matthew 13:45; 1 Corinthians 12:27)

We are committed to a vision of justice, peace and human flourishing for the city and all its inhabitants.
(Amos 5:24; Amos 9:13-15)

We are committed to uncluttered church, focused on mission, rooted in local culture and equipping all to develop and use their God-given gifts.
(1 Corinthians 9:22; Romans 12:6-8)

We are committed to unconditional service, holistic ministry, bold proclamation, prioritising the poor and being a voice for the voiceless.
(Proverbs 19:17; Romans 12:1)

We are committed to respecting and building relationship with other faith communities and averse to all forms of manipulation or erosion of liberty.
(Matthew 22:37-40; Luke 10:30-37)

Humility

We acknowledge our dependence on God and affirm

our continual need of prayer and God's empowering Spirit.
(Proverbs 3:5; Mark 10:14-15; Ephesians 5:18)

We believe that all people are loved by God, regardless of age, gender, education, race or class, and that God works through all believers – and others besides.
(Galatians 3:28)

We respect others working alongside us in the inner city and are grateful for the foundations laid by the many who have gone before us.
(1 Corinthians 3:5-9, 1 Corinthians 16:15-18)

We want to learn from others, seeking to shape what we do in light of the experiences, discoveries, successes and mistakes of fellow-workers.
(Ecclesiastes 12:11; Romans 15:14; Colossians 3:16)

We are careful not to drain other local churches of their often limited resources, but hope to be an encouragement and support to them.
(Hebrews 10:25, 1 Corinthians 14:12)

We realise the importance of living uncluttered lives, holding possessions lightly and recognising that all we have is to be at God's disposal.
(Luke 12:32-34)

We know we are not indispensable and what we attempt

to do is part of a much bigger picture, so will try to keep ourselves in perspective.
(Romans 12:3-5)

Creativity

We recognise the importance of taking risks and the demands of mission in the inner city, and we believe that it is acceptable to fail.
(Hebrews 11:32-40)

We value courage, creativity and diversity as we try to discover relevant ways of being church in different contexts.
(Joshua 1:6-9)

We believe that questions and theological reflection are important as we learn together and so discern the way forward.
(Jude 17-23, 1 Peter 3:15)

We aim to be catalysts, encouraging and releasing creativity in both church and community as we seek and share God in the inner city.
(Mark 4:26-29)

We believe in discouraging dependency and developing indigenous leadership within maturing churches that will have the capacity to sustain and reproduce themselves.
(Acts 14:23)

We are excited that God can be discovered in the heart of the city and commit ourselves to explore various forms of prayer and worship that are appropriate here.
(Hebrews 10:19-25; Revelation 21:1-4)

We realise that God's Spirit blows freely and so we will not assume our work should continue indefinitely.
(John 3:7-8)

Relationship

We believe that, in Jesus, God is revealed locally, and that we should be committed to our local community or relational network and active members of it.
(John 1:14, 1 John 1:1)

We believe that the gospel works through relationships and that serving God consists largely in building life-giving relationships with others.
(1 Thessalonians 2:8)

We recognise that Christian faith is a journey and we are committed to helping people move forward, wherever they are at present.
(1 Corinthians 3:1-2)

We focus on under-churched areas and neglected people, trying to find ways of communicating Jesus appropriately to those most frequently marginalised, condemned and abused by society.
(James 1:27)

We challenge the trend of some Christians moving out of the cities and encourage Christians to relocate to the inner cities.
(Matthew 9:9-12)

We believe in doing things with and not just for communities, sharing our lives with others and learning from others who share their lives with us.
(1 Thessalonians 1:5-6)

We see teamwork, networking and mutual accountability as vital, recognising that individuals and churches need each other.
(Ephesians 4:11-13; Acts 2:42-46)

Appendix B: Get involved

Join in

If reading this book has got you thinking about getting involved with incarnational urban mission we would love to talk with you further.

Perhaps you would like to join an existing team or Christian community pioneered by Urban Expression. You can check out the current locations on our website, but new places are always being added, so get in touch to find out where the opportunities are.

Perhaps you would like to lead or join a new team. We have ideas of where we would like to send new teams but are also open to suggestions by those who feel called to other urban priority areas. Get in touch and we can explore this together.

There are Urban Expression sister agencies in the following places, so please get in touch directly with them to explore opportunities there.

Britain: www.urbanexpression.org.uk
www.facebook.com/Urban3xpression
@urbanshalom

The Netherlands: www.urbanexpression.nl
                     @urbanXpressioNL

Sweden: www.urbanexpression.se
           www.facebook.com/UrbanExpressionSverige

North America: www.urbanexpression.org

Support

Perhaps you feel inspired to help practically, prayerfully or financially?

To get our regular newsletter please drop us a line at enquries@urbanexpression.org.uk

To make a donation please use our paypal button at www.urbanexpression.org.uk/getinvolved/support

or write to us at:

Urban Expression
PO Box 35238
London
E1 0YZ
United Kingdom

Learn

- Crucible Course

The Crucible Course is a training programme developed by Urban Expression and friends.

It is for Jesus followers with courage and imagination, who suspect that:
> We live in a mission context and need to think like missionaries.
> We need to think creatively about church in diverse and changing cultures.
> We serve the God who constantly does new things on the margins.

If this sounds like you, come and join us. For more information visit www.cruciblecourse.org.uk

- The Conspirers Podcast

Occasionally some of us from like-minded agencies get together to share our mutual foolishness on all things urban and record it for all to hear!

The Conspirers Podcast is a series of conversations exploring issues of urban mission in Britain. It is offered as a resource to anyone seeking to deepen their understanding of incarnational ministry in disadvantaged communities. Conspirators around the table have so far included Andy Turner, Matt Wilson, Helen Sidebotham, Derek Purnell, John Hayes, Tim Evans and myself.

You can download and listen to these free podcasts by searching for The Conspirers Podcast on iTunes

Links

There are other agencies who share a commitment to the urban poor and inspire us along the way. Here are some of those we relate to. You can contact them for information about opportunities to serve with them too.

Servants to Asia's Urban Poor	www.servantsasia.org
Urban Vision	www.urbanvision.org.nz
Inner Change	www.innerchange.org
614	www.614network.com
Urban Presence	www.urbanpresence.org.uk
Urban Neighbours of Hope	www.unoh.org
Eden Network	www.eden-network.org
BMS World Mission	www.bmsworldmission.org

BIBLIOGRAPHY

Bakke, R. *A Theology as Big as The City* (IVP, 1997)
Bosch, D. *Transforming Mission* (Orbis, 1993)
Cray, G. *Discerning Leadership* (Grove Books, 2010)
Donovan, V.J. *Christianity Rediscovered, An Epistle from the Masai* (SCM, 1978)
Duckworth, J. and Duckworth, J. *Against the Tide, Towards the Kingdom* (Cascade Books, 2011)
Duffett, C. and Goddard, S. *Big Hearted* (Gilead, 2012)
Frost, M. *Exiles* (Hendrickson, 2006)
Goodhew, D. (Ed) *Church Growth In Britain: 1980 To the Present* (Ashgate, 2012)
Jones, O. *CHAVS: The Demonization of The Working Class* (Verso, 2011)
Kilpin, J. and Murray, S. *Church Planting in the Inner City: The Urban Expression Story* (Grove Books, 2007)
McFague, S. *Super, Natural Christians: How we should love nature* (London: SCM, 1997)
Murray, S. *Church After Christendom* (Paternoster, 2004)
Vanier, J. *Community and Growth* (DLT, 1979)

www.ingramcontent.com/pod-product-compliance
Lightning Source LLC
Chambersburg PA
CBHW070249230426
43664CB00014B/2458